AMAZING INVENTORY OF INCREDIBLE KNOWLEDGE

PUB TIME

TRIVIA

Publications International, Ltd.

Written by Christopher Lagerstrom & Jill Oldham

Cover photo: Shutterstock.com

Louis Weber, CEO
Publications International, Ltd.
7373 North Cicero Avenue
Lincolnwood, Illinois 60712

ISBN-13: 978-1-4508-7825-8
ISBN-10: 1-4508-7825-3

Manufactured in Canada

8 7 6 5 4 3 2 1

CONTENTS

TRIVIA TIME

Welcome to *Pub Time Trivia*. This is not your typical trivia book. If you're looking for dry and dusty historical trivia, you won't find it here. But if you think you know—or always wanted to know—the world's most unusual vending machine products, where to find the most poisonous animal in the world, how Google got its name, and many more attention-grabbing facts, you've come to the right place.

Pub Time Trivia is organized by topic, making it easy for you to pick your favorite category. Perhaps you win the office Oscar pool every year and would like to premiere with Movie Mania. Or you could tempt yourself with Food & Drink, or find out about Famous Firsts. You'll find questions on the right-hand pages and answers on the back of each page, along with a few extra tidbits that may teach you a thing or two.

Are you ready? Pull up a barstool, pull out *Pub Time Trivia*, and tell your friends the next trivia champion has arrived.

1. WHICH OF THESE DOG BREEDS CANNOT BARK?

A. Azawakh

B. Basenji

C. Catalburun

D. Mudi

2. INSECT STINGS KILL BETWEEN 40 AND 100 AMERICANS EVERY YEAR. BUT IN OTHER PARTS OF THE WORLD, BUGS KILL MANY TIMES THAT NUMBER. WHICH OF THESE CRITTERS IS RESPONSIBLE FOR THE MOST HUMAN DEATHS?

A. Assassin bug

B. Japanese beetle

C. Mosquito

D. Tsetse fly

1.

B. Basenjis, a favorite dog of ancient Egyptians, are incapable of barking. Instead, you'll hear them uttering a sound called a yodel. Azawakhs (African sight hounds), catalburuns (Turkish pointers that are readily identified by their "split-nose"), and mudis (Hungarian herding dogs) all make themselves heard with traditional barks.

2.

C. Believe it or not, mosquitoes are responsible for more deaths than any other creature in the world. They spread a wide variety of potentially deadly diseases, including malaria, which kills an estimated one million people a year.

3. WHAT IS A CAPON?

A. A castrated rooster

B. A pygmy giraffe

C. A wild dog

D. An unfertilized eagle egg

4. WHAT PART OF A HORSE IS KNOWN AS THE "FROG"?

A. Chest

B. Head

C. Hoof

D. Tail

5. WHAT TYPE OF ANIMAL IS A HOLSTEIN?

A. Cow

B. Horse

C. Pig

D. Sheep

6. TRUE OR FALSE?

The sting from a killer bee can be fatal.

3.

A. Ouch. Why would a rooster be castrated? To improve the tenderness and quality of its meat. Capon is known as a luxury food.

4.

C. The frog is the triangular mark on the bottom of a horse's hoof.

5.

A. Got milk? Black-and-white (or sometimes red-and-white) Holsteins are the most popular dairy cows in the United States, making up 90 percent of the total herd.

6.

True. Africanized honeybees, as killer bees are officially known, are extremely aggressive. They often attack in swarms, and their stings can kill. They are notorious for being easy to provoke and hard to escape. They will chase humans for great distances, and they've been known to stay angry for up to 24 hours.

7. **WHICH SPECIES CONTAINS THE MOST POISONOUS ANIMAL IN THE WORLD?**

A. Butterfly

B. Frog

C. Snake

D. Spider

8. **MOST PEOPLE KNOW THAT A GROUP OF LIONS IS CALLED A PRIDE AND A GROUP OF FISH IS CALLED A SCHOOL, BUT CAN YOU MATCH THESE ANIMALS WITH THEIR COLLECTIVE GROUP NAMES?**

1. Apes	**A.** Murder
2. Crows	**B.** Parliament
3. Jellyfish	**C.** Pod
4. Owls	**D.** Shrewdness
5. Ravens	**E.** Smack
6. Whales	**F.** Unkindness

9. **WHAT IS STORED INSIDE A CAMEL'S HUMP?**

7.

B. Dart poison frogs are the most poisonous animals in the world. The golden poison frog is so toxic that it's dangerous to even touch it. Just one golden poison frog has enough toxin to kill ten people. So if you find yourself in Central or South America, you might want to think twice before kissing that frog.

8.

1. D; 2. A; 3. E; 4. B; 5. F; 6. C.

9.

Fat. If you thought the answer was water, you're not alone. (You're wrong, but you're not alone.) The fat stored in a camel's hump allows the animal to go for up to a month without food—pretty useful for those long treks across the desert.

10. WHICH OF THE FOLLOWING ANIMALS WAS NEVER A RESIDENT OF THE WHITE HOUSE?

A. Alligator

B. Bobcat

C. Ostrich

D. Pygmy hippopotamus

11. MACARONI, GENTOO, CHINSTRAP, AND ROCKHOPPER ARE TYPES OF WHAT?

A. Butterflies

B. Dogs

C. Penguins

D. Zebras

12. WHICH OF THE FOLLOWING IS NOT A TYPE OF CAT?

A. Calico

B. Rex

C. Saluki

D. Scottish Fold

10.

C. The White House has been home to all sorts of animals—domesticated and otherwise. John Quincy Adams owned a gator that lived in the East Room for two months. Calvin Coolidge literally had a zoo at the White House, including a bobcat, a pygmy hippo, a bear, lion cubs, raccoons, a hyena, and more. Theodore Roosevelt had an extensive menagerie too.

11.

C. There are 17 breeds of penguins in the world; these are just four of them.

12.

C. Salukis are dogs—in fact, theirs may be the oldest known breed of domesticated dog. Salukis were held in such great esteem in ancient Egypt that they were sometimes mummified along with the pharaohs.

13. OF THE 12 SIGNS OF THE ZODIAC, HOW MANY ARE MODELED ON ANIMALS?

14. WHAT DO SNAKES PRIMARILY USE THEIR TONGUES FOR?

A. Hearing

B. Seeing

C. Smelling

D. Tasting

15. ON AVERAGE, WHICH OF THE FOLLOWING SHARK SPECIES KILLS THE MOST HUMANS EACH YEAR?

A. Copper shark

B. Bull shark

C. Tiger shark

D. Mako shark

13.

Seven. Aries (ram), Taurus (bull), Cancer (crab), Leo (lion), Scorpio (scorpion), Capricorn (sea goat), and Pisces (fish) are animal signs.

14.

C. While snakes can use their tongues for tasting and even touching, they use them mostly for smelling.

15.

B. The United States averages fewer than one shark fatality every two years, while an average of 39 people are killed each year by lightning strikes. Statistically, you should be more afraid of the turf than the surf.

16. **THE PANGOLIN, A TOOTHLESS MAMMAL FOUND IN SOUTHERN AFRICA AND ASIA, IS THE ONLY MAMMAL TO HAVE WHICH OF THE FOLLOWING REPTILIAN CHARACTERISTICS?**

A. Can grow back its tail

B. Has scales

C. Is cold blooded

D. Secretes venom

17. **EXCLUDING INSECTS, WHICH ANIMAL HAS THE FASTEST METABOLISM?**

A. Cheetah

B. Pygmy shrew

C. Hummingbird

D. Chipmunk

18. **TRUE OR FALSE?**

A jellyfish has no brain.

16.

B. The pangolin, sometimes referred to as the scaly anteater, is the only mammal with scales. It has no teeth, and uses its powerful claws to tear open termite and ant mounds.

17.

C. Hummingbirds, which consume more than their own body weight in nectar daily, are always mere hours away from starvation. With an average heart rate of 1,260 beats per minute, a hummingbird can slow its heart down to 50 to 180 beats per minute, allowing it to survive when food is scarce. Second place in the high metabolism race goes to the eternally hungry Eurasian pygmy shrew, which can go only ten minutes without eating.

18.

True. The jellyfish has no brain, blood, or nervous system. Jellyfish do have eyespots that can detect light and dark, as well as chemosensory pits that can identify potential predators. And don't let their name fool you—jellyfish are 95% water.

19. WHICH ONE OF THESE FROG SPECIES
IS ABLE TO CONTINUOUSLY FREEZE
AND THAW THROUGHOUT THE WINTER,
IN ORDER TO HIBERNATE UNDER
SURFACE LEAVES?

A. Wood frog

B. Waxy monkey frog

C. Purple frog

D. Western spotted frog

20. MOST PEOPLE BELIEVE THAT SANTA'S
REINDEER ARE A SUBSPECIES OF THE
BULL REINDEER. BOTH BULL REINDEER
SEXES CAN GROW ANTLERS—BUT ON
CHRISTMAS EVE, WHICH SEX WOULD
SANTA'S REINDEER MOST LIKELY BE?

21. WHICH OF THESE SPECIES IS RESPONSIBLE
FOR THE MOST HUMAN FATALITIES ON THE
CONTINENT OF AFRICA?

A. Lion

B. Crocodile

C. Elephant

D. Hippopotamus

19.

A. Wood frogs are able to tolerate the extreme cold in their blood and other tissues, which allows them to freeze and thaw many times each winter as needed. Frogs also have the ability to breathe through their skin underwater, allowing oxygen to diffuse directly into their blood stream. No word on whether a kiss from an ice princess would make a frozen wood frog human or not, but don't hold your breath.

20.

Female. According to the Alaska Department of Fish and Gaming, male bull reindeer shed their antlers in October, while female bull reindeer don't shed their antlers until April.

21.

D. The male hippopotamus actively protects its territory, and females are known for aggressive behavior when their young are present. And hippos can run at speeds of up to 20 miles per hour. Next trip to Africa, pack your running shoes!

22. WHICH MARSUPIAL CAN GIVE BIRTH TO MORE LIVE BABIES THAN ANY OTHER SPECIES?

A. Kangaroo

B. Tasmanian devil

C. Koala

D. Possum

23. WHICH OF THE OBJECTS LISTED IS CLOSEST IN SIZE TO THE GIANT SQUID'S EYE, THE LARGEST EYE IN THE ANIMAL KINGDOM?

A. Baseball

B. Basketball

C. Bass drum

D. Monster-truck tire

24. VERY FEW MAMMALS ARE POISONOUS, BUT ONE OF THESE IS. WHICH ONE?

A. Beaver

B. Sloth

C. Kangaroo

D. Platypus

19

22.

B. After a 21-day gestation cycle, the Tasmanian devil can give birth to as many as 30 live young at one time. But because a mama Tasmanian devil has only four teats, her babies compete fiercely for milk. Eventually, Mom ends up eating many of her kids...whole. Aren't you glad you only got sent to your room?

23.

B. The giant squid's eye needs to be this large so it can detect one of its main predators, the sperm whale. The largest giant squid on record was 43 feet long. Not until 2004 did researchers acquire the first photo evidence of a giant squid in the wild.

24.

D. Along with laying eggs, the platypus has a spur on its hind foot that can deliver venom capable of causing severe pain in humans.

1. **WHICH INVENTOR ACTED AS A TUTOR TO HELEN KELLER, THE YOUNG GIRL WHO COULD NOT SEE, HEAR, OR SPEAK?**

A. Alexander Graham Bell

B. Thomas Edison

C. Antonio Meucci

D. Elisha Gray

2. **IN ROALD DAHL'S CHILDREN'S BOOK OF THE SAME NAME, TO WHAT DOES *THE BFG* REFER?**

A. Belly Flop Gang

B. Best Friends Guild

C. Brain Freeze Gulp

D. Big Friendly Giant

1.

A. Keller went on to dedicate her autobiography *The Story of My Life* to the man who invented the first practical telephone, the metal detector, and the hydrofoil.

2.

D. Standing 24 feet tall, the BFG's main job was to deliver good dreams to children. He first appeared in Dahl's *Danny, the Champion of the World*. Too bad he didn't show up in Dahl's James Bond script *You Only Live Twice*.

3. **WHICH OF THE FOLLOWING CHARACTERS NEVER APPEARED IN J.R.R. TOLKIEN'S *THE LORD OF THE RINGS* TRILOGY?**

A. Meriadoc

B. Ahsoka

C. Faramir

D. Elrond

4. **WHAT DISTINGUISHES FRENCH PAINTER MONET FROM FRENCH PAINTER MANET, ASIDE FROM THE VOWEL IN THEIR NAMES? MATCH EACH FACT TO ONE OF THE PAINTERS.**

A. Painted outdoor scenes and people while in a studio

B. Painted what he saw while outdoors

C. Was married twice and tried to commit suicide in between marriages

D. Married his father's mistress and died from rheumatism, gangrene, and syphilis

3.

B. Meriadoc was the Hobbit better known as Merry, Faramir was the human Boromir's brother, and Elrond was the elf lord. Ahsoka is Anakin Skywalker's apprentice in the TV show *Star Wars: The Clone Wars*...and maybe the future movies?

4.

Claude Monet was fond of painting outdoor scenes (**B**) and was married twice (**C**); Monet tried to end it all because he wasn't making money, but at the end of his life he did all right for himself. Edouard Manet primarily painted while indoors (**A**) and had an unpleasant demise (**D**); it's even possible that Manet's son might actually have been his brother.

5. **RICHARD BACHMAN IS THE ALTER EGO OF WHICH FAMOUS AUTHOR?**

A. Stephen King

B. John Grisham

C. Tom Wolfe

D. John Updike

6. **IN RAY BRADBURY'S *FAHRENHEIT 451*, BOOKS ARE SO ILLEGAL THAT, IF YOU'RE FOUND WITH ONE, FIREFIGHTERS WILL BURN DOWN YOUR HOUSE. WHICH OF THESE BOOKS DIDN'T RAY BRADBURY WRITE?**

A. *Dandelion Wine*

B. *The Martian Chronicles*

C. *The Door into Summer*

D. *Something Wicked This Way Comes*

7. **WHAT DOES THE "J" STAND FOR IN AUTHOR J. K. ROWLING'S NAME?**

A. Jane

B. Joanne

C. Joely

D. Judy

5.

A. King chose the name Richard after crime novelist Donald E. Westlake's pseudonym, Richard Stark, and Bachman for the band Bachman-Turner Overdrive. He started writing under the pen name to test whether it was his talent or his name that sold books. He wrote four novels (*Rage*, *The Long Walk*, *Roadwork*, and *The Running Man*) before being discovered. King continues to reference his most lifelike creation to this day.

6.

C. *The Door into Summer* was written by Bradbury contemporary Robert A. Heinlein in 1956. Bradbury's seasonally titled *Farewell Summer* was published in 2006; Bradbury passed away six years later. Farewell, Ray.

7.

B. The initials stand for Joanne Kathleen, but the *Harry Potter* author usually goes by "Jo."

8. *DESTINO* IS A WALT DISNEY-PRODUCED ANIMATED SHORT FILM RELEASED IN 2003. ITS ACTUAL PRODUCTION BEGAN IN 1945 AND FEATURED WORK BY DISNEY HIMSELF AND WHAT FAMOUS ARTIST?

A. Salvador Dali

B. Pablo Picasso

C. Henri Matisse

D. Max Ernst

9. WHO SCULPTED THE FAMOUS STATUE DAVID, SUPPOSEDLY THE REPRESENTATION OF THE IDEAL MALE BODY?

A. Botticelli

B. Michelangelo

C. Francesco da Sangallo

D. Leonardo da Vinci

10. WHICH AUTHOR CREATED THE LAND OF OZ?

A. Roald Dahl

B. J.R.R. Tolkien

C. L. Frank Baum

D. C. S. Lewis

ARTS & LITERATURE

8.

A. While preparing for *Fantasia 2000*, Walt's nephew Roy E. Disney stumbled across the unfinished project and championed its completion. Disney added computer animation alongside the original footage. It's a meeting of the generations. A true Surrealist moment. It was…*Destino*.

9.

B. Take that, Mike "the Situation." You may think you have abs of steel, but David has equally well-sculpted abs of marble—and he's more than 500 years old.

10.

C. Oz stemmed from Baum's imagination, but the other writers also created some pretty fantastical worlds: Dahl came up with Willy Wonka's chocolate factory (among others), Tolkien is responsible for Middle-earth of *Lord of the Rings*, and Lewis dreamed up Narnia.

ANSWERS

28

11. ARCHITECT ANTONI GAUDÍ WAS CONSIDERED A *MODERNISTA*. HE WAS INSPIRED BY THE SHAPES OF TREE TRUNKS AND HUMAN BONES AS WELL AS THE CLASSIC GOTHIC STYLE, AND HE INCORPORATED ALL THREE INTO HIS DESIGNS. IN WHICH COUNTRY WILL YOU FIND HIS WORK?

A. France

B. Spain

C. Turkey

D. Italy

12. OPRAH WINFREY FAMOUSLY GOT INTO A FIGHT WITH WHICH AUTHOR ON HER TALK SHOW?

A. Dave Eggers

B. Jonathan Franzen

C. James Frey

D. Jonathan Safran Foer

13. WHICH BOOK USES EXACTLY 50 DIFFERENT WORDS?

11.

B. Do one of two things immediately. Check out the amazing photographs of his buildings online—or fly to Barcelona, Spain.

12.

C. When Oprah discovered that the author of the self-purported memoir *A Million Little Pieces* had lied about parts of his life in the novel, she was outraged. She said she felt "duped" and proceeded to give him a very public verbal whoopin'.

13.

Dr. Seuss's *Green Eggs and Ham*. Seuss's editor bet him he couldn't write a book using 50 words or less. Guess what? The editor lost.

14. WHICH AMERICAN POP ARTIST IS KNOWN FOR HIS PAINTINGS THAT RESEMBLE LARGE COMIC STRIPS?

A. Keith Haring

B. David Hockney

C. Roy Lichtenstein

D. Andy Warhol

15. HOW DID LEGENDARY PLAYWRIGHT TENNESSEE WILLIAMS (*A STREETCAR NAMED DESIRE*, *CAT ON A HOT TIN ROOF*) DIE?

A. He choked on a bottlecap.

B. He drowned in the Mississippi River.

C. He fell from a sixth-story window.

D. He was stabbed.

16. WHICH 20TH-CENTURY NOVELIST WAS KNOWN TO MANY BY THE NAME "PAPA"?

A. Truman Capote

B. William Faulkner

C. Ernest Hemingway

D. Kurt Vonnegut

14.

C. All four are leaders of the pop art movement, but only Lichtenstein created oversize paintings in the style of bold and bright traditional comic strips.

15.

A. Tennessee Williams, who battled alcoholism and depression for much of his life, died in 1983 at age 71 as a result of choking on the cap from a bottle of eyedrops.

16.

Ask not for whom the bell tolls; it tolls for (**C**), Ernest Hemingway, one of the best-known and most successful novelists of the 20th century. His works include *A Farewell to Arms*, *To Have and Have Not*, and, yes, *For Whom the Bell Tolls*, among others.

17. WHO DESIGNED THE GUGGENHEIM MUSEUM IN NEW YORK CITY?

A. Frank Gehry

B. Louis Kahn

C. Ludwig Mies van der Rohe

D. Frank Lloyd Wright

18. ON WHICH SURFACE WOULD YOU FIND A TRADITIONAL FRESCO?

A. A canvas

B. A piece of pottery

C. Skin

D. A wall

19. MATCH THESE ARTISTS WITH THE MOVEMENT WITH WHICH THEY ARE MOST ASSOCIATED:

1. Salvador Dali   **A.** Cubism

2. Henri Matisse   **B.** Impressionism

3. Claude Monet   **C.** Pop Art

4. Pablo Picasso   **D.** Fauvism

5. Andy Warhol   **E.** Surrealism

33

17.

D. The renowned modern-art museum showcased both Wright's affinity for the natural world and his later take on modernist architecture. It opened in 1959, after the death of both Wright and art collector Solomon Guggenheim.

18.

D. A fresco (which means "fresh" in Italian) is a mural painted on fresh, wet plaster with natural pigments. As the plaster and paint dry, the fresco hardens and becomes permanent. Frescoes are commonly found on church walls.

19.

1. E; 2. D; 3. B; 4. A; 5. C.

20. WHICH CHARACTER IS NOT FOUND IN *ALICE IN WONDERLAND*?

A. The Mad Hatter

B. The Mock Turtle

C. Tweedledum and Tweedledee

D. The White Witch

21. ACCORDING TO GREEK LEGEND, WHAT WAS LEFT IN PANDORA'S BOX AFTER SHE OPENED IT, RELEASING MISERY AND EVIL INTO THE WORLD?

A. Faith

B. Hope

C. Innocence

D. Trust

22. WHAT COLOR IS THE ARTS AND LITERATURE WEDGE IN THE GAME TRIVIAL PURSUIT?

20.

D. Alice encountered the Mad Hatter, the Mock Turtle, and Tweedledum and Tweedledee on her travels through Wonderland. To bump into the White Witch, she would have needed to take a detour to the land of Narnia.

21.

B. Tricky Zeus. The king of gods gave Pandora a box (well, technically it was a jar, but why quibble?) and warned her never, ever to open it. Of course he knew her curiosity would get the better of her, and indeed it did. Fortunately she was able to slam the lid shut while hope still remained.

22.

Brown. (Talk about trivial trivia!)

23. WHO WROTE *PRIDE AND PREJUDICE*?

A. Jane Austen

B. Elizabeth Bennet

C. Charlotte Brontë

D. Emily Brontë

24. WHICH OF THE FOLLOWING WAS NOT A PEN NAME OF SAMUEL CLEMENS (MARK TWAIN)?

A. W. Epaminondas Adrastus Blab

B. Sergeant Fathom

C. Thomas Jefferson Snodgrass

D. Milcent Mollins Stanwix

23.

A. Austen wrote the widely beloved novel. The Brontë sisters contributed *Jane Eyre* (Charlotte) and *Wuthering Heights* (Emily) to the genre. Elizabeth Bennet is a figment of Austen's imagination—the main character in *Pride and Prejudice*.

24.

D. The 19th-century humorist looked at life with a keen wit, and he never took himself too seriously either, as can be seen in his choice of aliases.

1. WHICH U.S. PRESIDENT FIRST CHOSE TO FLY IN A PRIVATE U.S. AIR FORCE PLANE INSTEAD OF ON COMMERCIAL AIRLINES?

A. Harry S. Truman

B. John F. Kennedy

C. Franklin D. Roosevelt

D. Dwight D. Eisenhower

2. WHO WAS THE FIRST PERSON BORN IN THE AMERICAS TO ENGLISH PARENTS?

A. John Truth

B. Virginia Dare

C. Sarah Delaware

D. John Maine

1.

C. The practice of using a private U.S. Air Force plane for the president of the United States was instituted in 1943, after concerns arose over the president's security while flying commercial. The president's plane, known today as *Air Force One*, was originally called *Sacred Cow*. The name had to be changed in 1953 after the president's plane shared airspace with a commercial airliner going by the same call sign.

2.

B. Virginia Dare, the first baby born in the Americas to English parents, was born in the Roanoke Colony in present-day North Carolina. Virginia's birth is known only because her grandfather, John White, returned to England for fresh supplies and spread the news of his new granddaughter. Upon his return to Roanoke, he discovered that the entire colony, including his granddaughter, had mysteriously disappeared.

3. **WHO WAS MAJOR LEAGUE BASEBALL'S FIRST ROOKIE OF THE YEAR?**

3. WHO WAS MAJOR LEAGUE BASEBALL'S FIRST ROOKIE OF THE YEAR?

A. Lou Gehrig

B. Babe Ruth

C. Honus Wagner

D. Jackie Robinson

4. WHICH MUSICIAN WAS FIRST TO HAVE A NUMBER-ONE HIT ON THE BILLBOARD HOT 100 FOR A SONG THAT FEATURED ONLY PIANO AND VOCALS?

A. Billy Joel

B. Elton John

C. Mariah Carey

D. Adele

5. WHO WAS THE COVER MODEL OF THE FIRST ISSUE OF *PLAYBOY* MAGAZINE (1953)?

A. Brigitte Bardot

B. Sophia Loren

C. Jayne Mansfield

D. Marilyn Monroe

3.

D. In 1947, Jackie Robinson won the very first Rookie of the Year award. The award was originally called The J. Louis Comiskey Award after the longtime owner of the Chicago White Sox. The award was renamed The Jackie Robinson Award in 1987, 40 years after Jackie Robinson suited up as a Brooklyn Dodger and broke baseball's color barrier.

4.

D. In 2011, Adele's "Someone Like You" became the first single ever to reach the number one spot on the charts with piano and vocals exclusively. "Candle in the Wind 1997," Elton John's tribute song to Princess Diana, topped the charts for 14 weeks in 1997—if it weren't for that pesky orchestra at the end.

5.

D. Monroe was also the centerfold of that issue.

6. WHAT 1970S FILM WAS THE FIRST TO FEATURE A COMPUTER-GENERATED TITLE SEQUENCE?

A. *Jaws 2*

B. *Revenge of the Pink Panther*

C. *Grease*

D. *Superman*

7. WHO WAS *TIME* MAGAZINE'S VERY FIRST MAN OF THE YEAR?

A. Mahatma Gandhi

B. Adolf Hitler

C. Charles Lindbergh

D. Albert Einstein

8. WHICH SHOW WAS THE FIRST EVER TO WIN A TONY AWARD FOR BEST MUSICAL?

A. *Kiss Me, Kate*

B. *South Pacific*

C. *Guys & Dolls*

D. *The King and I*

6.

D. *Superman* became the first of many films to use computer animation in its opening sequence. Released in 1978, *Superman*'s production preceded a boom in digital filmmaking by only a few years (the CGI-heavy *Tron* was released in 1982). As such, the film's creative team had to manufacture a 70-foot scale model of the Golden Gate Bridge, as well as one for the Hoover Dam.

7.

C. Charles Lindbergh was an easy pick for the first *Time* magazine Man of the Year in 1927—and not just because *Time* forgot to put him on its cover earlier that year when he completed the world's first transatlantic flight.

8.

A. The first Tony Awards were given out in 1947, but until 1949, there was no category for Best Musical. In 1949, *Kiss Me, Kate*, based on William Shakespeare's *The Taming of The Shrew*, took the inaugural honors for a new musical. New rule: "If you want an award, always bet on Shakespeare."

9. **WHICH WAS THE FIRST RECURRING CHARACTER TO BE KILLED OFF BY THE MAKERS OF LONG-RUNNING ANIMATED TV SERIES *THE SIMPSONS*?**

A. Maude Flanders

B. Sideshow Bob

C. Bleeding Gums Murphy

D. Dr. Julius M. Hibbert

10. **THE FIRST CREDIT CARD WAS INTRODUCED IN NEW YORK IN 1950. WHAT WAS IT?**

A. American Express

B. BankAmericard

C. Diners Club

D. MasterCard

11. **THE FIRST MOVING PICTURE COPYRIGHTED IN AMERICA SHOWED WHAT?**

A. An automobile racing a horse

B. A lady crossing a street

C. A man sneezing

D. Two people kissing

9.

C. After long debates about offing a character, the makers of *The Simpsons* finally pulled the trigger in Season Six, when they killed off Lisa Simpson's idol, jazz musician Bleeding Gums Murphy. Bleeding Gums Murphy appeared to Lisa one last time in the form of a speaking cloud, alongside Darth Vader of *Star Wars* and Mufasa from *The Lion King*, characters originally voiced by James Earl Jones, who reprised his roles for the cartoon.

10.

C. Although the American Express company was established a century before Diners Club, it specialized in deliveries (as a competitor to the U.S. Postal Service), money orders, and traveler's checks. It didn't enter the credit card industry until 1958.

11.

C. The five-second movie, filmed in 1894 by the Edison Manufacturing Company (yes, that Edison— he did a lot more than invent the lightbulb), showed Edison's assistant Fred Ott taking a pinch of snuff and sneezing. Five stars!

12. SEEING A NEED FOR A STORE WHERE YOU COULD BUY MILK, BREAD, AND EGGS AFTER REGULAR GROCERY STORES CLOSED FOR THE NIGHT, "UNCLE" JOHNNY JEFFERSON GREEN OPENED THE VERY FIRST AFTER-HOURS CONVENIENCE STORE, WHICH EVOLVED INTO A CHAIN OF STORES KNOWN WORLDWIDE AS 7-ELEVEN. WHAT DID GREEN ORIGINALLY CALL HIS STORE?

A. Uncle Johnny's Icehouse

B. Tote'm

C. Stop and Go

D. Jefferson General

13. WHAT WAS THE FIRST ITEM SOLD ON EBAY?

A. Answering machine

B. Calculator

C. Computer keyboard

D. Laser pointer

12.

B. Tote'm stores were named for how customers could simply buy goods and "tote 'em" away. Many of the first Tote'm stores even had original Alaskan totem poles out front. In 1946, the chain changed its name to 7-Eleven to let customers know about their newly extended hours.

13.

D. eBay was founded in 1995 by Pierre Omidyar, whose broken laser pointer was the first product to be auctioned off (reportedly for about $14). The buyer was aware it was broken—he wanted it as an addition to his collection of broken laser pointers. True story.

14. WHO WAS THE FIRST HUMAN IN SPACE?

A. Yuri Gagarin

B. John Glenn

C. Alan Shepard

D. German Titov

15. WHAT WAS THE FIRST ANIMATED FILM TO BE NOMINATED FOR AN ACADEMY AWARD FOR BEST PICTURE?

A. *Aladdin*

B. *Beauty and the Beast*

C. *The Lion King*

D. *The Little Mermaid*

16. WHAT WAS MICKEY MOUSE'S ORIGINAL NAME?

A. Malachi Mouse

B. Marvin Mouse

C. Milton Mouse

D. Mortimer Mouse

14.

A. The Russian cosmonaut launched aboard the *Vostok 1* on April 12, 1961, and orbited the Earth once. The spacecraft was controlled from the ground for the duration of the 108-minute flight. Gagarin was its only passenger.

15.

B. *Beauty and the Beast* was nominated in 1991 but was beaten out by *The Silence of the Lambs*. However, it did win the Golden Globe for Best Picture (Musical or Comedy) that year—the first full-length animated feature to claim that prize.

16.

D. Walt Disney created Mortimer Mouse in 1928. The name was short-lived, however; supposedly Disney's wife thought it sounded too pompous and suggested "Mickey" as a replacement.

17. *SATURDAY NIGHT LIVE* PREMIERED ON OCTOBER 11, 1975. WHO WAS ITS FIRST-EVER CELEBRITY HOST?

A. Desi Arnaz

B. Candice Bergen

C. George Carlin

D. Bob Newhart

18. CAN YOU MATCH THE CELEBRITY WITH HIS FIRST-EVER TWEET?

1. Bill Cosby

2. Danny DeVito

3. Tom Hanks

4. Neil Patrick Harris

5. Ashton Kutcher

A. dropping my first tweet

B. Have a tweet time and I will write tweet nothings in your ear.

C. I just joined Twitter! I don't really get this site or how it works. My nuts are on fire.

D. My first tweet, peeps. I apologize in advance for my slow learning curve. Nice to (sort of) meet you. It's amazing how quickly 140 charac

E. Testing...Testing...Is this thing on?

51

17.

C. Unlike today's guest hosts, who appear in most of the show's sketches, Carlin only appeared onstage to perform stand-up comedy and introduce the musical guests.

18.

1. B; 2. C; 3. E; 4. D; 5. A.

19. WHAT WAS THE FIRST COLLEGE FOUNDED IN THE UNITED STATES?

A. College of William and Mary

B. Harvard University

C. University of Pennsylvania

D. Yale University

20. WHAT WAS THE FIRST SELECTION FOR OPRAH'S BOOK CLUB?

A. *The Deep End of the Ocean* (Jacquelyn Mitchard)

B. *Here on Earth* (Alice Hoffman)

C. *Song of Solomon* (Toni Morrison)

D. *White Oleander* (Janet Fitch)

21. WHAT WAS THE FIRST VIDEO EVER PLAYED ON MTV?

A. "Beat It," Michael Jackson

B. "Money for Nothing," Dire Straits

C. "Paradise by the Dashboard Light," Meat Loaf

D. "Video Killed the Radio Star," The Buggles

19.

B. Harvard was called "New College" when it was founded in 1636. Technically, Henricus Colledge was chartered first (in Virginia in 1619), but it was a casualty of the Indian uprising of 1622.

20.

A. Thanks to Oprah's influence, Mitchard's book became a national bestseller within four months of its publication.

21.

D. At midnight on August 1, 1981, MTV launched with the airing of the music video of the Buggles' 1979 debut single. Irony at its finest.

22. WHICH FIRST LADY WAS A DISTANT COUSIN OF HER HUSBAND?

23. WHICH TEAMS PLAYED IN THE FIRST SUPER BOWL?

   A. Green Bay Packers and Oakland Raiders

   B. Green Bay Packers and Kansas City Chiefs

   C. Baltimore Colts and New York Jets

   D. Minnesota Vikings and Kansas City Chiefs

24. WHERE WAS THE WORLD'S FIRST STARBUCKS?

   A. Portland, Oregon

   B. San Francisco, California

   C. Seattle, Washington

   D. Vancouver, Canada

25. WHICH IS THE FIRST BOOK IN THE *HARRY POTTER* SERIES?

   A. *Harry Potter and the Chamber of Secrets*

   B. *Harry Potter and the Goblet of Fire*

   C. *Harry Potter and the Prisoner of Azkaban*

   D. *Harry Potter and the Sorcerer's Stone*

22.

Eleanor Roosevelt. She and FDR were fifth cousins once removed.

23.

B. The first Super Bowl, called the AFL–NFL World Championship Game, was played in February 1967. The Green Bay Packers beat the Kansas City Chiefs 35–10.

24.

C. Although today it may seem like there's a Starbucks on every corner, there was a time when you would have had to travel to Seattle to get your morning fix. When it opened in 1971, the store didn't even sell coffee by the cup; it sold small batches of fresh-roasted coffee.

25.

D. If you're European, you probably know the book as *Harry Potter and the Philosopher's Stone*. Its U.S. publisher decided to rename it to emphasize the magic and wizardry—"philosopher" just didn't have the same pizzazz.

1. BEFORE BECOMING BABY RUTH IN 1921, WHAT WAS THE CANDY BAR'S ORIGINAL NAME?

A. Nuts N' Nougat

B. The ChocoBar

C. Caramel Surprise

D. Kandy Kake

2. WHEN HOSTESS DECLARED BANKRUPTCY IN 2012, THE FUTURE FOR TWINKIES DIDN'T LOOK SO CREAMY. WHICH COMPANY HAS SAVED THE GOLDEN CAKE FROM BECOMING HISTORY?

A. Nabisco

B. Apollo

C. Little Debbie

D. Pepperidge Farm

1.

D. Already successful in Chicago, the Curtiss Candy Company thought the redesigned bar needed a new name. The company claimed the change had nothing to do with Babe Ruth's rise in fame. They claimed it was named after President Grover Cleveland's daughter, Ruth. Cleveland had been president 30 years prior, and his daughter Ruth had passed away in 1904 at the age of 12. A clever marketing move to get around licensing, or simple truth? It didn't matter to Nabisco, who bought the company 60 years later, or Nestlé, who owns them today.

2.

B. One of these things is not like the other. Apollo is a global management firm that owns the likes of AMC Entertainment, Norwegian Cruise Lines, and Carl's Jr. Hopefully, with Apollo's help, Twinkies *can* last forever.

3. WHAT IS THE ONLY FOOD THAT, WHEN SEALED, DOESN'T SPOIL?

A. Beer nuts

B. Capers

C. Fruit preserves

D. Honey

4. TRUE OR FALSE?

It takes seven years to digest swallowed gum.

5. THE MCDONALD'S BIG MAC IS BY FAR THE CHAIN'S BIGGEST HIT. BUT STANDING IN STARK CONTRAST TO THAT SANDWICH ARE SOME WACKY OFFERINGS. WHICH OF THESE WAS NOT A REAL MENU ITEM FROM THE FAST-FOOD BEHEMOTH?

A. McCrepe

B. McGratin Croquette

C. McLobster

D. McPizza

3.

D. Airtight containers will make honey last forever—literally! Several giant vats of honey, untouched for more than 3,000 years, were excavated from King Tut's tomb. Incredibly, the honey was found to still be edible.

4.

False. Although gum is indigestible, it passes through your digestive system at a normal rate.

5.

A. You won't find a crepe on any Mickey D's menu past or present, but the other three have all been featured at some point. What's in a McGratin Croquette, you ask? The Japanese-market sandwich featured fried macaroni, shrimp, and mashed potatoes. Are you lovin' it?

6. WHAT DOES THE SCOVILLE SCALE MEASURE?

A. The fattiness of a cut of meat

B. The purity of olive oil

C. The "heat" of chilies

D. The clarity of wine

7. M&MS AND GATORADE COME IN A RAINBOW OF COLORS THANKS TO MYRIAD ARTIFICIAL DYES. RESEARCHERS HAVE FOUND THAT ONE OF THESE COLORS OF DYES MAY HELP CURE SPINAL CORD INJURIES. DO YOU KNOW WHICH ONE?

8. ACCORDING TO THE U.S. FOOD AND DRUG ADMINISTRATION (FDA), MOST RAW FRUITS AND VEGETABLES ARE COMPLETELY FAT-FREE. WHICH IS THE EXCEPTION TO THIS RULE?

A. Bananas

B. Broccoli

C. Jicama

D. Plums

6.

C. Are you feeling hot, hot, hot? The Scoville scale can either confirm or refute your hotness.

7.

Blue. Researchers discovered that an injection of the dye Brilliant Blue G halted the chemical reaction that destroys spinal tissue after an injury. Better yet, after the dye was injected into rats paralyzed from spinal cord injuries, they were able to walk again. The only side effect? They temporarily turned blue.

8.

B. If you zeroed in on broccoli, you're correct. While the others have zero fat, broccoli has a whole—*gasp*—.5 grams per stalk. (Still pretty healthy, no? Doesn't that make you want to put down those nachos and Buffalo wings?)

9. WHICH PRODUCT WAS ORIGINALLY MARKETED AS "ESTEEMED BRAIN TONIC AND INTELLECTUAL BEVERAGE"?

A. Coca-Cola

B. Maxwell House coffee

C. Schweppes ginger ale

D. Smart Water

10. CLAMSHELL, TABLE, BLACK TRUMPET, AND GOLDEN NEEDLE ARE ALL TYPES OF WHAT?

A. Figs

B. Mushrooms

C. Pears

D. Snails

11. WHICH OF THESE SWEET TREATS HAS NOT BEEN FEATURED AS A MAIN INGREDIENT IN A BREAKFAST CEREAL?

A. AirHeads

B. Ice cream

C. Raisinets

D. Willy Wonka's Nerds candy

9.

A. Coca-Cola was invented in Atlanta, Georgia, where it debuted in 1886 and sold for five cents a glass.

10.

B. If you see any of these varieties, feel free to yell, "There's a fungus among us!" (Although people might look at you funny.)

11.

C. Although sugar-happy tykes everywhere might think Raisin Bran could be improved by coating the raisins with chocolate, no such cereal has been created...yet. Cap'n Crunch's AirHeads Berries was produced by Quaker in 2003. In 1965 Kellogg's introduced Kream Krunch, which was filled with bits of freeze-dried ice cream. And the tangy flavor of Nerds candy was recreated in Nerds Cereal in the mid-1980s, with Ralston cleverly dividing the cereal box in half to feature a different flavor in each compartment, just like the candy box.

12. Each year, people celebrate local food specialties with giant festivals. If you're tired of the same old chili cook-off or apple pie contest, you may want to check one of these out. All but one is a real festival—which is the odd man out?

A. Jelly Jam-boree

B. Turkey Testicle Festival

C. Waikiki SPAM Jam West

D. Virginia Roadkill Cook-off

13. True or false?

Eating turkey makes people sleepy.

14. Natural vanilla flavoring comes from which flower?

A. Calla lily

B. Dahlia

C. Orchid

D. Sweet pea

12.

A. If you find yourself with a craving for some turkey testicles, drop by Huntley, Illinois, in November. For roadkill delicacies, head to Pocahontas County, West Virginia, in September. And if you like canned meat, you're in luck—every April. Alas, if you're looking to sample jellies and jams, you may have to start your own festival.

13.

False. Turkey contains tryptophan—an amino acid that makes people sleepy—but it doesn't work unless it's consumed in large quantities.

14.

C. Vanilla pods, or beans, are the fruit of the vanilla orchid—the only orchid plant that produces an edible fruit. Now, if only chocolate grew on trees... Wait a minute—it does! Cacao pods, which are used to make chocolate, grow on small tropical trees called Theobroma cacao trees.

15. AMERICANS DRINK 13 BILLION GALLONS OF SOFT DRINKS EVERY YEAR. WHICH OF THE FOLLOWING IS NOT A REAL PRODUCT?

A. DraCola

B. EpilepsiPepsi

C. Leninade

D. Whooppee Soda

16. WHAT IS THE ONLY ROCK THAT IS EDIBLE FOR HUMANS?

17. TOFU (OR *DOUFU*, AS IT WOULD MORE ACCURATELY BE SPELLED IN CHINA) IS A STAPLE OF ASIAN COOKING, AND IT HAS MADE INROADS IN NORTH AMERICAN CUISINE BECAUSE OF ITS HIGH PROTEIN AND CALCIUM CONTENT. IT IS MADE FROM SOYBEANS; IN FACT, *DOU* MEANS "BEANS." BUT WHAT DOES THE *FU* TRANSLATE AS?

A. Curd

B. Rotten

C. Silk

D. Vegan

FOOD & DRINK

QUESTIONS

15.

B. There's no such thing as EpilepsiPepsi. The other three were all actual soft drinks. DraCola was a cola product made for "Halloween fans of all ages" by Transylvania Imports. Leninade was humorously promoted with slogans like, "A taste worth standing in line for," and "A drink for the masses!" And Whooppee Soda was a ginger ale–flavored soda marketed as "The Bottled Joy."

16.

Salt. The mineral is essential to the body, but consuming too much is not good for you. No surprise there. But did you know that it can be deadly? An overdose of salt was a traditional method of suicide in ancient China.

17.

B. Mmmm-mm, "rotten beans." No wonder tofu has a bad rap!

ANSWERS

18. HORSE NETTLE, AN INGREDIENT SOMETIMES FOUND IN TEA, BOASTS WHICH OF THE FOLLOWING BENEFITS?

A. Acne combatant

B. Laxative

C. Pick-me-up

D. Sedative

19. SURVEY SAYS: AMERICA'S FAVORITE PIZZA TOPPING IS PEPPERONI. WHICH OF THESE INGREDIENTS IS COMMONLY FOUND ON PIZZA IN JAPAN?

A. Cucumber

B. Mayonnaise

C. Pickled ginger

D. Rice

20. WHICH OF THE FOLLOWING HAS NOT BEEN PRODUCED AS A JELLY BELLY FLAVOR?

A. Bloody Mary

B. Denver Omelet

C. Pickle

D. Sausage

18.

D. Horse nettle actually has nothing to do with horses, so PETA members have nothing to worry about. You might, though—horse nettle is a flowering weed whose unripe fruit is poisonous. The ripe fruit is not harmful, however, and when cooked it has mild sedative powers. Don't try this at home, kids!

19.

B. Squid, seaweed, corn, and bacon are also common toppings in Japan, and you'll even find delicacies like a mini–hot dog pizza on a Japanese Pizza Hut menu.

20.

B. The other three have been rolled out as "specialty" flavors—although "special" may not be the word that comes to mind after tasting them. Pickle and Sausage are found in Bertie Bott's Every Flavor Beans, and Bloody Mary was a prototype "rookie" flavor that's no longer produced. What a shame!

1. WHICH AUTOMAKER CREATED THE ANDROID ASIMO?

A. Kia

B. Toyota

C. Honda

D. Nissan

2. WHAT IS THE NAME OF THE HERO IN MOST INSTALLMENTS OF THE FOLLOWING VIDEO GAME FRANCHISES?

A. *Halo* (XBOX)

B. *Metal Gear Solid* (Playstation)

C. *The Legend of Zelda* (Nintendo)

D. *Uncharted* (Playstation)

1.

C. ASIMO stands for Advanced Step in Innovative MObility. Sure, it can walk and even run 3.7 mph, but have you seen the video of it falling on a set of stairs? We're talking RoboTube comedy gold... assuming that's what robots call their version of YouTube.

2.

A. Master Chief; **B.** Solid Snake; **C.** Link; **D.** Nathan Drake. There are the most Zelda games (at least 15, not counting re-releases). Halo is hot on Zelda's heels with seven. Snake and Drake have only seen four games each, but as we've all learned, you can't keep a good guy down.

3. HOW LONG IS A "SCORE" OF YEARS?

A. 4 years

B. 7 years

C. 20 years

D. 80 years

4. HOW MANY MILLIONS MAKE UP A TRILLION?

5. HOW LONG DOES IT TAKE SUNLIGHT TO REACH EARTH?

A. 8 seconds

B. 8 minutes

C. 8 hours

D. 8 days

6. WHAT DOES A PLUVIOMETER MEASURE?

A. Cell tower strength

B. Hurricane strength

C. Radiation level

D. Rainfall amount

3.

C. Have you always wondered what Abraham Lincoln meant by "four score and seven years ago"? He was referring to the signing of the Declaration of Independence in 1776, which occurred 87 years—four score and seven years—before the 1863 Gettysburg Address.

4.

There are one million millions in a trillion.

5.

B. Traveling at the speed of, well, light, sunlight reaches our atmosphere eight minutes after leaving the sun.

6.

D. For when you want to know whether you should wear your Wellies or not.

7. WHERE DID GOOGLE GET ITS NAME?

A. It's the name of a galaxy discovered in 1998, the year the company was founded.

B. It's a variation of the term googol, a very large number (1 followed by 100 zeroes).

C. It's a type of sponge (symbolic of an ability to absorb large amounts of information).

D. It's gibberish; the founders of Google came up with the word after having a few cocktails.

8. WHICH OF THESE SUPERHEROES DEBUTED FIRST?

A. Batman

B. Hulk

C. Spider-Man

D. Superman

9. HOW MANY LETTERS OF THE ALPHABET ARE USED IN THE ROMAN NUMERAL SYSTEM?

A. 6

B. 7

C. 8

D. 9

7.

B. The amount of information that can be found with this search engine makes even a googol look small. Maybe we should upgrade to a googolplex—ten to the googol power!

8.

D. Superman arrived from the planet Krypton in 1938. Batman was hot on his heels in 1939, but Spider-Man and the Hulk didn't make their debuts until 1962.

9.

B. VII letters are used: I=1, V=5, X=10, L=50, C=100, D=500, and M=1,000.

10. WHICH PLANET IN OUR SOLAR SYSTEM HAS THE LONGEST DAY?

A. Earth

B. Jupiter

C. Mercury

D. Venus

11. WHAT COLOR IS PAC-MAN?

12. NOBEL PRIZES ARE AWARDED IN SIX FIELDS. HOW MANY CAN YOU NAME?

13. WHICH OF THE FOLLOWING IS THE CHEMICAL SYMBOL FOR IRON?

A. Fe

B. Ir

C. Tn

D. Zn

10.

D. In fact, a day on Venus (equal to 243 Earth days) is longer than its year (225 Earth days).

11.

Yellow

12.

Physics, chemistry, medicine or physiology, literature, peace, and economic science.

13.

A. It's short for the Latin word *ferrum*.

14. **WHO IS THE FIRST CHARACTER TO SPEAK IN THE MOVIE *STAR WARS*?**

15. **WHAT DOES HE OR SHE SAY?**

16. **CAN YOU MATCH THESE MYTHICAL HYBRIDS WITH THEIR DESCRIPTIONS?**

1. Centaur

2. Chimera

3. Minotaur

4. Satyr

5. Sphinx

A. Head and legs of a bull, torso of a man

B. Head and torso of a man, legs of a goat

C. Head and torso of a man, body of a horse

D. Head of a woman, body of a lion

E. Part lion, part goat, part serpent

17. **WHO WAS THE FOUNDER OF SCIENTOLOGY?**

A. Arthur C. Clarke

B. Enrico Fermi

C. Stephen Hawking

D. L. Ron Hubbard

79

14.

C-3PO, the droid with the snazzy gold paint job, speaks first.

15.

"Did you hear that?" (He's talking to R2-D2, and "that" is the sound of the main reactor being shut down on Princess Leia's ship.)

16.

1. C; 2. E; 3. A; 4. B; 5. D.

17.

D. Scientology has enticed thousands into its fold, though the sheer number of high-profile celebrities might make you guess higher.

18. INKY, BLINKY, AND PINKY ARE THREE OF PAC-MAN'S FOUR ENEMIES. WHO IS THE FOURTH?

A. Clinky

B. Clyde

C. Dinky

D. Steve

19. AT WHAT TEMPERATURE DOES PAPER BURN?

A. 451°F

B. 507°F

C. 666°F

D. 800°F

20. THE TURBO PC, THE FIRST PERSONAL COMPUTER, WAS DESIGNED BY WHAT MANUFACTURER IN 1985?

A. Acer

B. Packard Bell

C. Dell

D. Gateway

GEEKERY

ANSWERS

18.

B. Clyde is the orange ghost. Blinky is red, Inky is blue, and Pinky is, well, pink.

19.

A. So if you accidentally put the frozen pizza in the oven with its cardboard backing, you should be okay—as long as the temp is 450° Fahrenheit or lower. (Still, it's best to pay attention and follow the directions, no?)

20.

C. Founder Michael Dell dropped out of college to found PCs Limited, which would quickly become Dell Computer Corporation, and eventually Dell Inc. The Turbo PC sold for $795, and after one year in business, Michael Dell's company had grossed more than $73 million. Stay in school, shmay in school.

21. WHY IS FACEBOOK'S LAYOUT DESIGN BLUE?

A. The color is easier on the eyes than other colors, allowing users to spend more time on the site.

B. Facebook founder Mark Zuckerberg is colorblind.

C. Blue is the only color Zuckerberg knew how to code during Facebook's initial development.

D. Blue is Zuckerberg's favorite color.

22. AS APPLE DEVELOPED THE POWER MAC 7100 IN THE EARLY 1990S, IT USED THE NAME OF A FAMOUS ASTRONOMER AS A CODE NAME. WHO WAS THE ASTRONOMER?

A. Albert Einstein

B. Edwin Hubble

C. Carl Sagan

D. Clyde Tombaugh

21.

B. More specifically, he is red–green colorblind, and blue is the most vibrant color he can see.

22.

C. Sagan sued the company over the use of his name (and lost), but Apple decided to change the code name anyway, to "BHA." What did BHA stand for, you ask? "Butt-head astronomer."

GRAB BAG

1. **ALTHOUGH IT'S RARE ON EARTH, WHAT IS THE SECOND-MOST ABUNDANT ELEMENT IN THE KNOWN UNIVERSE?**

2. **AN INTERROBANG IS MADE BY COMBINING WHAT TWO PUNCTUATION MARKS?**

   A. ! and ?

   B. > and <

   C.) and (

   D. : and %

3. **WHAT SYMBOL IS ALSO KNOWN AS AN OCTOTHORPE?**

4. **LIST ALL EIGHT VEGETABLES IN THE ORIGINAL RECIPE FOR V8 JUICE.**

1.

Helium. Earth is running out of helium, which is mostly mined from the ground. Helium conservationists seek to multiply its price by 20 times to stop wasteful use. Look out, gold, there's a new precious commodity in town—save those birthday balloons!

2.

A. Invented in 1962 by advertiser Martin Spektor, the combination expresses surprise in a question. Through the early 1970s, the key could be found on typewriters or as an add-on, but the fad faded away like a forgotten pet rock.

3.

You may know it as the pound, number, or hashtag sign. For the record, the asterisk (*) is also known as a sextile.

4.

Beets, carrots, celery, lettuce, parsley, spinach, tomatoes, and watercress.

5. A 2013 DOCUMENTARY ENTITLED *SIRIUS* IS ABOUT THE ATACAMA HUMANOID DISCOVERED IN A DESERT IN CHILE IN 2003. WHAT'S SO UNIQUE ABOUT THE HUMANOID NICKNAMED ATA?

A. It has a full-length, prehensile tail.

B. It's been fully preserved for more than 500 years.

C. It's six inches tall.

D. It has wings instead of arms.

6. LEGO BRICKS WERE INTRODUCED IN WHAT DECADE?

A. 1930s

B. 1940s

C. 1950s

D. 1960s

7. MOUND METALCRAFT, FOUNDED IN 1946, CHANGED ITS NAME IN 1955, AND ITS NEW NAME BECAME SYNONYMOUS WITH A CERTAIN TYPE OF TOY TRUCK. WHAT WAS THE COMPANY'S NEW NAME?

87

5.

C. Are you Sirius? The public has speculated that Ata is an extraterrestrial, but DNA testing determined it's human after all.

6.

C. LEGO creator Ole Kirk Christansen named his wooden toys factory after a fusion of the Danish words "leg" and "godt," literally meaning "play well." The plastic bricks were perfected in the 1950s, and a new LEGO brick will fit one made in 1958. I guess you could say they still stack up against themselves.

7.

Tonka. The name came from the Dakota Sioux word tanka, meaning "great" or "big." Tonka has almost become a proprietary eponym, like Xerox or Kleenex, when referring to toy trucks.

8. WHICH IS THE ONLY KING CARD IN A STANDARD DECK OF PLAYING CARDS WITHOUT A MOUSTACHE?

A. King of Diamonds

B. King of Hearts

C. King of Spades

D. King of Clubs

9. WHAT IS THE STATUE OF LIBERTY'S OFFICIAL NAME?

A. Lady Liberty on the Isle

B. Light of Liberty, Let It Shine

C. Liberty Gertrude Ellis

D. Liberty Enlightening the World

10. WHAT IS NOT A POSSIBLE ANSWER FROM THE MAGIC 8-BALL?

A. As I see it, yes

B. Better not tell you now

C. I don't think so

D. Without a doubt

8.

B. Because he also holds his sword behind (or through) his head, the King of Hearts is also called the suicide king. Did you know that each card represents a famous king? The King of Diamonds is Julius Caesar or Caesar Augustus, Clubs is Alexander the Great, Spades is King David of Israel, and Hearts is Charlemagne.

9.

D. Given to us by France in 1886, she's become quite the movie star. At her worst, she's appeared in such features as *Independence Day*, *The Day After Tomorrow*, *Judge Dredd*, *A.I.*, *X-Men*, *Cloverfield*, and of course, *Planet of the Apes*. At her best: *Sabotage*, *Men in Black II*, *The Adjustment Bureau*, and of course, *Ghostbusters II*.

10.

C. There are 20 answers on the Magic 8-Ball's icosahedron die (which has 20 sides), and only five of them are negative: "Don't count on it," "My reply is no," "My sources say no," "Outlook not so good," and "Very doubtful."

11. WHICH OF THE FOLLOWING IS NOT A REAL BEAUTY PAGEANT?

A. Miss Klingon Empire

B. Miss Artificial Beauty

C. The Armpit Queen

D. Miss Michael Jackson

12. HOW MANY BATHROOMS DOES THE WHITE HOUSE HAVE?

A. 22

B. 35

C. 50

D. 57

13. WHAT IS THE MOST COMMONLY REPORTED SUBJECT OF PEOPLE'S DREAMS?

A. Being chased

B. Falling/flying

C. Missing/failing an exam

D. Sex

11.

D. The Miss Klingon Empire beauty pageant is held every September at Dragon*Con in Atlanta. A Miss Artificial Beauty pageant was held in Beijing, China, in 2004; each contestant had to present doctor-certified proof of her surgical enhancements. Old Spice deodorant sponsors an annual pageant and festival in Battle Mountain, Nevada, which was once dubbed "the armpit of America" by humorist Gene Weingarten of the Washington Post. Sweaty T-shirt contests, deodorant throws, and a "quick-draw" antiperspirant contest lead up to the selection of the Armpit Queen.

12.

B. Encompassing approximately 55,000 square feet, the White House has 132 rooms, including 35 bathrooms and 16 family and guest rooms.

13.

A. It's often interpreted as symbolic of feeling as though you are being pursued by events or unpleasant emotions in your daily life.

14. WHAT IS THE BEST-SELLING CAR OF ALL TIME?

15. JUPITER, MARS, MERCURY, NEPTUNE, PLUTO, AND VENUS ARE—OR WERE— PLANETS. (SORRY, PLUTO.) WHAT ELSE DO THESE NAMES HAVE IN COMMON?

16. WHICH IS NOT CONSIDERED ONE OF THE SEVEN HOLY VIRTUES?

A. Charity

B. Faith

C. Fortitude

D. Patience

17. WHAT IS DONALD DUCK'S MIDDLE NAME?

A. Buzz

B. Chesterfield

C. Fauntleroy

D. Fitzgerald

14.

The Toyota Corolla. Since its 1966 debut, more than 37 million Corollas have been sold.

15.

Each is the name of a Roman god. Jupiter is the king of the gods; Mars is the god of war; Mercury is the messenger of the gods; Neptune is the god of the sea, earthquakes, and horses; Pluto is god of the dead and the Underworld; and Venus is the goddess of love and beauty.

16.

D. Whoever first uttered the adage "patience is a virtue" didn't know their holy virtues from a hole in the wall. The seven holy virtues are: faith, hope, charity, prudence, justice, temperance, and fortitude.

17.

C. "Fauntleroy" is a nice upper-class-sounding name, befitting a nephew of Scrooge McDuck, who has a fortune estimated at five billion impossibidillion fantasticatrillion dollars.

18. **BENJAMIN FRANKLIN IS A MEMBER OF 14 HALLS OF FAME. WHICH OF THE FOLLOWING IS NOT ONE OF THEM?**

A. Agricultural Hall of Fame

B. American Mensa Hall of Fame

C. International Swimming Hall of Fame

D. World Chess Hall of Fame

19. **THE JAPANESE SEEM TO HAVE A YEN FOR SELLING UNUSUAL PRODUCTS VIA VENDING MACHINE—THEY SELL MORE PRODUCTS THIS WAY THAN ANY OTHER COUNTRY. WHICH OF THESE IS NOT AVAILABLE FOR PURCHASE IN JAPANESE VENDING MACHINES?**

A. Designer condoms

B. Gasoline

C. Live rhinoceros beetles

D. Sake in preheated containers

20. **WHAT IS THE MAXIMUM NUMBER OF CHARACTERS ALLOWED IN A SINGLE TWEET?**

18.

A. Among Franklin's myriad interests and talents, he was an enthusiastic and well-trained swimmer. When he was just a boy, he strapped boards to his hands in an effort to swim faster, effectively inventing the hand paddles swimmers still use for training.

19.

B. In addition to live beetles (a popular pet for Japanese children), condoms, and warm drinks, Japanese vending machines have also been known to dispense fresh eggs, pornographic magazines, kerosene, and more. However, even though you may find a can of hot red beans for sale, one thing the vending machines won't give you is gas.

20.

140

21. ALFRED KINSEY, NOTED PIONEER OF SEX RESEARCH, SPENT YEARS INTERVIEWING THOUSANDS OF PEOPLE TO STUDY HUMAN SEXUALITY. HE FOUNDED THE INSTITUTE FOR SEX RESEARCH IN 1947 AT WHICH UNIVERSITY?

A. Indiana University

B. Northwestern University

C. The Ohio State University

D. University of Wisconsin

22. WHAT DO HOMER SIMPSON AND ELVIS PRESLEY HAVE IN COMMON?

23. HOW MANY ASTRONAUTS HAVE WALKED ON THE MOON?

A. 9

B. 12

C. 14

D. 15

21.

A. Kinsey and his staff collected more than 18,000 interviews at a time when discussing sexuality was very much taboo in America. Some hailed him as a liberator of sexuality; others (including Billy Graham) vilified him as the direct cause of declining morals in Americans.

22.

They both have daughters named Lisa Marie.

23.

B. Between July 20, 1969, and December 19, 1972, six Apollo missions landed on the moon. Altogether, 12 astronauts spent time on lunar soil.

24. TRUE OR FALSE?

The modern brassiere was invented by a man.

25. WHICH STAR HAS NOT BEEN TWICE-CROWNED SEXIEST MAN ALIVE BY *PEOPLE* MAGAZINE?

A. George Clooney

B. Tom Cruise

C. Johnny Depp

D. Brad Pitt

26. STELLA LIEBECK OF ALBUQUERQUE, NEW MEXICO, SUCCESSFULLY SUED McDONALD'S FOR GROSS NEGLIGENCE OVER WHAT 1992 INCIDENT?

A. Burned herself with hot coffee

B. Found a finger in her fries

C. Contracted salmonella poisoning from undercooked McNuggets

D. Slipped and fell on wet floor

24.

False. Bras were invented in 1913 when American socialite Mary Phelps-Jacob tied two handkerchiefs together with ribbon. She patented the idea a year later. Maidenform introduced modern cup sizes in 1928.

25.

B. Clooney (1997, 2006), Depp (2003, 2009), and Pitt (1995, 2000) have been anointed twice each, but Cruise has only earned the title once (1990).

26.

A. Liebeck, 79, burned herself so severely that she needed skin grafts. Two years later, a jury awarded her more than $2.5 million, which an appeals court later reduced to $480,000. The sides eventually settled out of court for an undisclosed amount.

1. WHAT WAS THE END RESULT OF THE MANHATTAN PROJECT?

A. An atomic bomb

B. The Brooklyn Bridge

C. A hovercraft

D. The flux capacitor

2. THE WAR OF 1812 OCCURRED BETWEEN WHICH TWO NATIONS?

A. France and Spain

B. Russia and the British Empire

C. The British Empire and the United States

D. France and Russia

3. OF THE CELEBRATED GREEK PHILOSOPHERS —ARISTOTLE, PLATO, AND SOCRATES— WHO TAUGHT WHOM?

1.

A. The project lasted from 1942 to early 1947 and took place simultaneously in more than 30 cities in the United States, Canada, and the United Kingdom. Manhattan was the first headquarters of the top-secret project—right across from city hall.

2.

C. All the above pairings were at war with each other in 1812, due to a little emperor named Napoleon. Ultimately, the 32-month Revolutionary War rematch resolved the remaining concerns over the United States' declaration of independence, and the U.S. and the U.K. have been close allies ever since.

3.

Socrates taught Plato, and Plato taught Aristotle. You can remember the order by the acronym "SPA." Just don't confuse SPA with SAP or ASP.

4. **WHICH TOWN WAS THE SCENE OF THE GUNFIGHT AT THE O.K. CORRAL?**

A. Cimarron, New Mexico

B. Cripple Creek, Colorado

C. Dodge City, Kansas

D. Tombstone, Arizona

5. **WHAT AGE FOLLOWED THE BRONZE AGE?**

A. Ice Age

B. Iron Age

C. Stone Age

D. Age of Innocence

6. **DURING THEIR EXPEDITION ACROSS THE AMERICAN WEST FROM 1804 TO 1806, EXPLORERS MERIWETHER LEWIS AND WILLIAM CLARK TRAVELED WITH A FRENCH FUR TRADER AND HIS YOUNG SHOSHONE WIFE. WHAT WAS HER NAME?**

A. Kateri Tekakwitha

B. Pocahontas

C. Sacagawea

D. Weetamoo

4.

D. Actually, the famous gunfight between Wyatt Earp's crew and a group of outlaw brothers took place near the O.K. Corral, in an empty lot next to Camillus Fly's photography studio. Perhaps "Gunfight at the C.F. Studio" wasn't catchy enough.

5.

B. Characterized by the types of material being used to make tools at the time, the Stone Age is first in the Three-Age System of archaeology, followed by the Bronze Age and then the Iron Age. In Hollywood, though *Ice Age* was followed by *Ice Age: The Meltdown, Ice Age: Dawn of the Dinosaurs*, and *Ice Age: Continental Drift*.

6.

C. Although she did not serve as a guide for the expedition, as is often reported, Sacagawea helped foster diplomacy with Native Americans, provided input on the best routes to take, and served as an interpreter. She was the human version of a modern smart phone.

7. HOW MANY WIVES DID KING HENRY VIII HAVE?

A. 5

B. 6

C. 7

D. 8

8. HALLEY'S COMET LAST APPEARED IN 1986. WHEN IS IT SCHEDULED TO APPEAR NEXT?

A. 2041

B. 2048

C. 2061

D. 2087

9. ACCORDING TO THE SUPREME COURT DECISION IN THE CASE OF *BROWN V. BOARD OF EDUCATION*, THE *PLESSY V. FERGUSON* DECISION VIOLATED WHICH AMENDMENT BY UPHOLDING RACIAL SEGREGATION IN PUBLIC SCHOOLS?

A. First Amendment

B. Eleventh Amendment

C. Twelfth Amendment

D. Fourteenth Amendment

7.

B. Henry was married six times. Probably the most famous of his wives was the ill-fated Anne Boleyn, executed in 1536. If you have trouble keeping track of all of Henry's wives, try to remember this little mnemonic device: "Annulled, beheaded, died; annulled, beheaded, survived."

8.

C. The comet is visible from Earth every 75 to 76 years as it orbits the Sun. American author Mark Twain was born two weeks after the comet's perihelion (when it's closest to the sun) in 1835, and he predicted he would live until the comet's return. He died April 21, 1910—the day after the comet's next perihelion.

9.

D. The Equal Protection Clause of the Fourteenth Amendment states, "No state shall...deny to any person within its jurisdiction the equal protection of the laws." The Fifteenth Amendment ultimately allowed everyone to vote. (Except women—that happened 50 years later.)

10. WHAT WAS THE NAME OF THE THEATER WHERE PRESIDENT LINCOLN WAS ASSASSINATED?

A. Booth Theater

B. Ford's Theater

C. Lions Theater

D. Marquee Theater

11. INVESTMENT MANAGER BERNIE MADOFF SHOCKED WALL STREET AND THE WORLD WHEN HE WAS ARRESTED FOR STEALING BILLIONS OF DOLLARS FROM INVESTORS IN A MASSIVE FINANCIAL FRAUD. WHAT KIND OF SCAM WAS THIS?

12. WHICH WAR DO THE MOVIES *APOCALYPSE NOW*, *FULL METAL JACKET*, *HAMBURGER HILL*, AND *PLATOON* DEPICT?

A. Vietnam War

B. Korean War

C. Peloponnesian War

D. Crimean War

10.

B. On the night of April 14, 1865, John Wilkes Booth waited for the main character's big laugh line in Tom Taylor's play *Our American Cousin*: "Don't know the manners of good society, eh? Well, I guess I know enough to turn you inside out, old gal—you sockdologizing old man-trap." The audience's laughter concealed the gunshot. It's probably inappropriate to say you had to be there.

11.

A Ponzi scheme. U.S. prosecutors estimated that the worldwide scheme eventually totaled $64.8 billion. Madoff pled guilty to 11 criminal charges, including wire fraud, mail fraud, and money laundering. In 2009, he was sentenced to 150 years in prison. Using that length of sentence, he'll repay his duped investors at a rate of $14 per second…if he somehow manages to live until 2159.

12.

A. Including *Good Morning, Vietnam* would have made it too easy.

13. ALCATRAZ ISLAND HAS A RICH HISTORY, BEGINNING WITH ITS NAME. ALCATRAZ IS A SPANISH WORD THAT TRANSLATES INTO WHAT?

A. Prison

B. Pelican

C. Paradise

D. Poet

14. WHEN ALLIED TROOPS INVADED THE BEACHES OF NORMANDY, FRANCE, ON JUNE 6, 1944, IT WENT BY WHAT CODENAME?

A. Operation Neptune

B. Operation Luna

C. Operation Phalanx

D. Operation Eclipse

15. WHAT DID AL CAPONE GO TO JAIL FOR?

A. Extortion

B. Mail fraud

C. Tax evasion

D. Murder

13.

B. Originally considered the "Evil Island" by Native Americans, the "Island of the Pelicans" has been a military garrison, a military prison, the site of a Native American civil rights occupation, and a tourist trap. Operating as a federal prison from 1934 to 1963, Alcatraz housed such notorious figures as Al Capone, Mickey Cohen, and George "Machine Gun" Kelly. Now it's home to the California slender salamander. At least those don't try to escape.

14.

A. Likely named for the Roman god of the sea, Operation Neptune succeeded after elaborate deceptions led Adolf Hitler to believe that Allied forces planned to attack from the Straits of Dover. That operation was called Operation Bodyguard. No guessing where that name came from!

15.

C. Despite all his alleged wrongdoings, he was only ever convicted of income tax evasion in 1931 and sentenced to 11 years in prison. Capone was paroled in 1939 and succumbed to a heart attack in 1947.

16. WHO FAMOUSLY SAID, "THAT'S ONE SMALL STEP FOR [A] MAN, ONE GIANT LEAP FOR MANKIND"?

A. Buzz Aldrin

B. Neil Armstrong

C. John Glenn

D. Buzz Lightyear

17. HOW LONG WAS THE SHORTEST WAR IN HISTORY?

A. 16 months

B. 24 weeks

C. 32 days

D. 40 minutes

18. WHO WAS THE ONLY PRESIDENT TO GET MARRIED IN THE WHITE HOUSE?

A. Martin Van Buren

B. Grover Cleveland

C. James A. Garfield

D. Warren G. Harding

16.

B. Armstrong was the first man to walk on the moon. Later that year, Apollo 12 astronaut Pete Conrad, shortest member of his astronaut corps, landed on the Moon, jumped down from his lunar module, and said, "Whoopie! That may have been a small one for Neil, but it's a long one for me."

17.

D. After the pro-British sultan of Zanzibar died in 1896, a not-so-pro-British sultan took his place. The United Kingdom issued an ultimatum that resulted in a 40-minute war. Zanzibar took 500 casualties while Britain took just one. Another pro-British sultan assumed leadership of the puppet government, and Britain controlled Zanzibar for the next 67 years.

18.

B. Another noteworthy "one and only" fact about the man on the $1,000 bill: He's the only president to serve two non-consecutive terms. Cleveland was the 22nd and 24th president of the United States of America.

19. WHAT FAMOUS WORLD EVENT HAPPENED ON NOVEMBER 9, 1989?

A. The TV show *Seinfeld* premiered.

B. The Berlin Wall fell.

C. Ayatollah Khomeini died.

D. The Tiananmen Square massacre occurred.

20. THE ROSETTA STONE IS AN IMPORTANT ARTIFACT BECAUSE IT ALLOWED HISTORIANS TO DO WHAT?

A. Map out pyramid interiors

B. Flatten wet papyrus

C. Translate ancient text

D. Find Mt. Olympus

19.

B. What a big year in history 1989 happened to be. All of the events above occurred in 1989, but the toppling of the Berlin Wall and reunification of Germany began on November 9. British Prime Minister Margaret Thatcher begged Soviet President Mikhail Gorbachev not to let it happen because she feared the worst for Europe.

20.

C. The carved stone contained text written in three different ancient languages. Using their knowledge of the Greek text, linguists were able to translate the stone's older Egyptian writings and hieroglyphs. Think of it as a 1,700-pound decoder ring: the original translator app.

HUMAN BODY

1. EVERYONE KNOWS NOT TO LEAVE FINGERPRINTS BEHIND IF THEY WANT TO KEEP THEIR IDENTITY UNREVEALED. WHAT OTHER BODY PART HAS A UNIQUE PRINT?

A. Nose

B. Tongue

C. Ear

D. Elbow

2. WHAT IS THE COLORED PART OF THE EYE CALLED?

A. Cornea

B. Iris

C. Pupil

D. Retina

1.

B. Yet another reason not to lick doorknobs.

2.

B. The most common eye color in the world is brown. The least common is green. So what's the bestselling colored contact lens, you wonder? There's no record of that, but it's probably not cat's eyes.

3. WHAT IS THE MOST COMMON BLOOD TYPE?

A. B+

B. O-

C. AB

D. O+

4. WHICH OF THESE IS A PIGMENT FOUND IN HUMAN SKIN THAT HELPS DEFEND AGAINST SUNBURN?

A. Mitochondria

B. Miasma

C. Methylene

D. Melanin

5. WHICH OF THE FOLLOWING BODY PARTS IS NO LONGER REQUIRED BY HUMANS?

A. Vermiform appendix

B. Wisdom teeth

C. Auriclares muscles

D. Semilunar folds

3.

D. However, the O- blood type is the universal donor, meaning all other blood types can mix with it. That's why TV and movie doctors so often call for "O Neg." But people who have O- blood can only receive O- blood, and they make up less than 8% of the total U.S. population. To get an A+ on this blood test, you should also know that AB- is the rarest blood type—less than 1% of the total U.S. population has it.

4.

D. Melanin is found in most living organisms, but one major exception is spiders. With or without melanin, spiders make some people's skin crawl!

5.

All of the above. The vermiform appendix was probably your first guess, but wisdom teeth (leftovers from the era in which people chewed more foliage), auriclares muscles (those that redirect your ears), and semilunar folds (the fold in the corner of the eye, a vestigial remnant of another eyelid) are all nonessential in modern humans.

6. HAIR COLOR DETERMINES HOW MUCH ACTUAL HAIR IS ON YOUR HEAD. PUT THESE NATURAL HAIR COLORS IN ORDER, FROM THE COLOR THAT MEANS THE LEAST HAIR TO THE COLOR THAT MEANS THE MOST: BLONDE, RED, BLACK, AND BROWN.

7. WHAT IS THE NAME OF THE BONE THAT EXTENDS FROM THE SHOULDER TO THE ELBOW?

A. Humerus

B. Lunate

C. Radius

D. Ulna

8. WHAT NUTRIENT DO WE ABSORB FROM EXPOSURE TO SUNLIGHT?

A. Calcium

B. Magnesium

C. Vitamin A

D. Vitamin D

6.

Red (around 90,000), brown (around 100,000), black (around 110,000), and finally blonde (around 140,000). The average amount of hair follicles on the human head is 100,000, and each follicle produces about 20 new strands over time, so if you're already bald, scold your follicles for spending those strands so carelessly.

7.

A. The humerus is also known as the funny bone, and that's no joke. That last sentence was a joke, though. Did it tickle your humerus? (Not to be confused with humor, which is the fluid that fills your eyeballs.)

8.

D. Hence vitamin D's nickname: the sunshine vitamin. If you're looking to amp up your vitamin D intake, turn to mushrooms, fatty fish, beef liver, or eggs. Intake means you're supposed to eat them— not bask in their glow.

9. TRUE OR FALSE?

Humans have only five senses.

10. WE BEGIN OUR LIVES WITH MORE THAN 300 BONES, BUT SOME OF THOSE 300 FUSE TOGETHER DURING GROWTH. HOW MANY BONES DO ADULTS HAVE?

A. 182

B. 206

C. 274

D. 302

11. IF YOU HAVE *MAL DE MER*, WHAT ARE YOU SUFFERING FROM?

A. The flu

B. Food poisoning

C. Seasickness

D. Vertigo

9.

False. And there isn't an agreed-upon number of them, either. Aside from the main five (sight, sound, touch, taste, and smell), some of the others include: proprioception (knowing where your body parts are in relation to other parts), equilibrioception (balance), nociception (pain), thermoception (temperature), and, of course, hunger and thirst.

10.

C. Good thing bones don't continue to fuse—we wouldn't be much more flexible than Barbie and Ken dolls.

11.

C. It's French for seasickness. *Mal* means "bad" or "ill"; *de mer* means "of the sea." Now hand me a bucket, *s'il vous plait*.

12. TRUE OR FALSE?

To cure severe diarrhea in some patients, doctors have resorted to transplanting donor fecal matter.

13. IN 1955, JONAS SALK DISCOVERED A VACCINE FOR WHAT DISEASE?

A. Polio

B. Measles

C. Mumps

D. Rubella

14. WHICH ORGAN PRODUCES INSULIN?

A. Kidney

B. Liver

C. Pancreas

D. Small intestine

15. WHAT SYMPTOM DOES *PILOERECTION* CAUSE?

A. Excessive blinking

B. Goosebumps

C. Impotence

D. Vomiting

123

12.

True. There's a bacterium called *Clostridium difficile* ("C. diff") that can overtake the intestines. The only way to restore the good bacteria required to defeat the bad is to use a healthy person's bacteria.

13.

A. Incredibly, Salk chose not to patent the vaccine. On his decision, Salk said: "There is no patent. Could you patent the sun?"

14.

C. Insulin is a hormone that moves sugar out of the blood and into the body's cells. You can think of it as a key that unlocks the door to the cell so that food (sugar/glucose) can get inside and feed it. A deficiency of insulin can lead to diabetes.

15.

B. *Piloerection* is an involuntary reflex that causes the muscles around the base of each hair follicle to contract, making the hairs stand up and causing small bumps to appear.

16. WHAT IS THE LARGEST ORGAN IN THE HUMAN BODY?

A. Brain

B. Lower intestine

C. Lungs

D. Skin

17. HOW MANY CHROMOSOME PAIRS CAN BE FOUND IN A HUMAN CELL?

A. 11

B. 16

C. 20

D. 23

18. WHERE IN OR ON YOUR BODY IS THE HALLUX FOUND?

A. Ear

B. Face

C. Foot

D. Reproductive organs

16.

D. The average person sheds nearly 1.5 pounds of skin per year. After 50 years, you'll have left 75 pounds of old skin lying around! Try and shed that image.

17.

D. Chromosomes are made of DNA. Half of your chromosomes come from your mother, the other half from your father. And it's the 23rd chromosome that determines your sex. One X always comes from Mom; X or Y comes from Dad. XX: it's a girl! XY: it's a boy! And the double helix of life rolls on and on.

18.

C. *Hallux* means big toe; *pollex* means thumb; *Horcrux* means you think too much about the Harry Potter books and films.

19. WHAT DOES REM STAND FOR?

20. WHICH OF THE FOLLOWING FACTS
ABOUT CRYING IS NOT TRUE?

A. Tears release toxins that reduce stress.

B. The scent of women's tears reduces
men's sexual arousal.

C. You can't cry with your eyes closed.

D. There are three types of tears.

19.

Rapid eye movement. When we sleep, we drift between rapid eye movement (REM) sleep and non-REM sleep in 90-minute cycles. During REM sleep, we have our most vivid dreams, characterized by bizarre plots involving unlikely people or things. Non-REM dreams are more like waking thoughts. If you thought this was a question about the band R.E.M., lead singer Michael Stipe has said that the band's name means nothing, and that it was picked randomly out of the dictionary...where the meaning above must've been plain as day.

20.

C. You practically can't sneeze with your eyes open, or effectively yawn (which cools down the brain, scientists say), but you can certainly cry with your eyes shut. And in case you're wondering, the three types of tears aren't crocodile, happy, and "of a clown." The real types are basal (lubricant), reflexive (when injured), and psych (emotional).

MOVIE MANIA

1. WHO IS ANGELINA JOLIE'S FAMOUS DAD?

A. James Caan

B. George Hamilton

C. Harvey Keitel

D. Jon Voight

2. WHO IS THE OLDEST ACTOR EVER TO WIN AN OSCAR?

A. George Burns

B. Kirk Douglas

C. Paul Newman

D. Christopher Plummer

3. SUPERSTAR ACTOR JOHNNY DEPP AND DIRECTOR TIM BURTON HAVE TEAMED UP ON EIGHT FILMS (SO FAR). HOW MANY OF THEM CAN YOU NAME?

1.

D. The two haven't always been on the best of terms, but they allegedly reconciled in 2010. Mom was actress Marcheline Bertrand.

2.

D. Plummer was 82 years old when he scored the Best Supporting Actor statuette for his role in the 2011 film *Beginners*.

3.

Edward Scissorhands (1990), *Ed Wood* (1994), *Sleepy Hollow* (1999), *Charlie and the Chocolate Factory* (2005), *Corpse Bride* (2005), *Sweeney Todd* (2007), *Alice in Wonderland* (2010), and *Dark Shadows* (2012).

4. **CAN YOU TELL WHICH OF THESE IS NOT THE TITLE OF A REAL MOVIE?**

A. *Cannibal Cousin and the Knife of Destiny*

B. *Sorority Babes in the Slimeball Bowl-O-Rama*

C. *Pumpkinhead II: Blood Wings*

D. *Mari-Cookie and the Killer Tarantula in 8 Legs to Love You*

5. **THE JAMES BOND SERIES IS FAMOUS FOR ITS GORGEOUS LEADING LADIES. CAN YOU MATCH THE BOND GIRL WITH THE MOVIE IN WHICH SHE APPEARED?**

1. *Goldfinger*   **A.** Jinx Johnson

2. *You Only Live Twice* **B.** Kissy Suzuki

3. *Quantum of Solace*   **C.** Pussy Galore

4. *Casino Royale*   **D.** Strawberry Fields

5. *Die Another Day*   **E.** Vesper Lynd

6. **WHAT IS THE ONLY X-RATED MOVIE EVER TO WIN AN ACADEMY AWARD FOR BEST PICTURE?**

131

4.

A. Actress Linnea Quigley, known as the "Queen of Scream," starred in the other three (1988, 1994, and 1998, respectively), among other piquantly titled horror thrillers. The titles may be more scream-worthy than the movies!

5.

1. C; 2. B; 3. D; 4. E; 5. A.

6.

Midnight Cowboy. The movie, starring Dustin Hoffman and Jon Voight, took home the prize in 1969. Because of the growing stigma associated with X ratings, the film's rating was changed to R in 1971 without anything being changed or removed.

7. THERE ARE MORE THAN 2,400 STARS ON THE HOLLYWOOD WALK OF FAME. WHICH OF THESE MAJOR HOLLYWOOD SUPERSTARS DOES NOT HAVE ONE?

A. Clint Eastwood

B. Harrison Ford

C. Arnold Schwarzenegger

D. John Travolta

8. IN *STAR WARS*, WHAT IS THE NAME OF HAN SOLO'S SPACECRAFT?

A. *Apollo*

B. *Enterprise*

C. *Millennium Falcon*

D. *Voyager*

9. IN THE *BACK TO THE FUTURE* FRANCHISE, AT WHAT SPEED IS THE DeLOREAN TIME MACHINE ACTIVATED?

A. 78 mph

B. 88 mph

C. 98 mph

D. 108 mph

7.

A. Go ahead—give Eastwood a star. It would probably make his day.

8.

C. The Falcon's design was allegedly inspired by a hamburger, with the cockpit being an olive on the side. Mmmm-mm. Hungry?

9.

B. Hello? McFly? Is anybody home? Of course you knew that the flux capacitor kicks into gear at 88 miles per hour.

10. **WHO PLAYED INDIANA JONES'S FATHER IN *INDIANA JONES AND THE TEMPLE OF DOOM*?**

A. Sean Connery

B. James Garner

C. Gene Hackman

D. Peter O'Toole

11. **WHICH OF THE FOLLOWING JULIA ROBERTS MOVIES WAS NOT BASED ON A TRUE STORY?**

A. *Charlie Wilson's War* (2007)

B. *Eat Pray Love* (2010)

C. *Erin Brockovich* (2000)

D. *Larry Crowne* (2011)

12. **WHICH FAMOUS *SATURDAY NIGHT LIVE* ALUM WROTE 2004'S HIT FILM *MEAN GIRLS*?**

A. Tina Fey

B. Ana Gasteyer

C. Amy Poehler

D. Maya Rudolph

10.

A. Yep, James Bond himself was also Indy's dad. Director Steven Spielberg thought Connery was an obvious choice for the role, as Bond was an inspiration for Indiana's character.

11.

D. Don't get Charlie Wilson confused with Larry Crowne. Both movies costarred Tom Hanks; only one of them was the story of a real person (Wilson).

12.

A. Gasteyer and Poehler each had a role in the film, but Fey wrote the script. Poehler played the mom of Rachel McAdams's mean-girl character, which was odd because in real life she's just seven years older than McAdams.

13. **MARILYN MONROE IN A BILLOWING WHITE DRESS OVER A SUBWAY GRATE—WHO DOESN'T KNOW THAT SCENE? BUT DO YOU KNOW WHAT MOVIE IT'S FROM?**

A. *Gentlemen Prefer Blondes*

B. *How to Marry a Millionaire*

C. *The Seven Year Itch*

D. *Some Like It Hot*

14. **WHICH OSCAR-NOMINATED ACTION STAR IS ALSO A SEASONED HELICOPTER PILOT AND REAL-LIFE HERO?**

A. Tom Cruise

B. Harrison Ford

C. John Travolta

D. Denzel Washington

15. **WHICH TWO ACTORS STARRED IN 2005'S *BROKEBACK MOUNTAIN*?**

13.

C. The pose is so famous, in fact, that it was commemorated with a 26-foot-tall statue on Chicago's Magnificent Mile. Sadly, the statue was only a temporary display.

14.

B. Ford has twice rescued stranded hikers in his Bell 407 helicopter. In July 2000 he airlifted a hiker off Table Mountain in Idaho, and a year later he rescued a 13-year-old Boy Scout who had gotten lost in Yellowstone Park.

15.

Jake Gyllenhaal and Heath Ledger. Both were nominated for Academy Awards.

16. **BRAT PACK MOVIES *THE BREAKFAST CLUB*, *FERRIS BUELLER'S DAY OFF*, AND *SIXTEEN CANDLES* (ALL DIRECTED BY JOHN HUGHES) WERE SET IN THE SUBURBS OF WHICH METROPOLIS?**

A. Boston

B. Chicago

C. Los Angeles

D. Philadelphia

17. **WHICH ACTOR PROVIDES THE VOICE OF *TOY STORY*'S BUZZ LIGHTYEAR?**

A. Tim Allen

B. Will Ferrell

C. Tom Hanks

D. Mike Myers

18. **WHICH ACTRESS PLAYED GERTIE IN THE MOVIE *E.T. THE EXTRA-TERRESTRIAL*?**

A. Drew Barrymore

B. Cameron Diaz

C. Gwyneth Paltrow

D. Reese Witherspoon

16.

B. It seems there was no place like home for Hughes, who grew up in Northbrook, Illinois, a suburb of Chicago.

17.

A. You're sure to recognize the other actors' voices from animated films as well: Will Ferrell plays Megamind, Tom Hanks is the voice of Buzz's pal Woody, and Mike Myers is Shrek.

18.

A. Barrymore was just seven years old when she starred in the blockbuster movie.

19. **IN 1999'S OFFICE SPACE, THE MEEK AND MUMBLY MILTON IS OBSESSED WITH WHICH OFFICE SUPPLY?**

A. Calculator

B. Scissors

C. Stapler

D. Wite-Out

20. **WHICH OF THE FOLLOWING ACTORS FROM THE *STAR WARS* FILM SERIES WAS A STEP-COUSIN TO IAN FLEMING, AUTHOR OF THE JAMES BOND NOVELS?**

A. Alec Guinness (Obi-Wan Kenobi)

B. Anthony Daniels (C-3PO)

C. Liam Neeson (Qui-Gon Jinn)

D. Christopher Lee (Count Dooku)

21. **TRUE OR FALSE?**

In *Friday the 13th Part II*, Jason Voorhees' mask was based on a 1950s Detroit Red Wings goalie mask.

19.

C. Milton's all about his Swingline stapler. Well, that and burning down the building.

20.

D. Lee's mother married into Fleming's family, but it was his acting that got him a part as the James Bond villain Scaramanga in *The Man with the Golden Gun*, right? Maybe. Lee was Fleming's regular golf partner after all. Do you think he ever golfed with George Lucas?

21.

False, but not for the reason you think. It *was* based on goaltender Terry Sawchuk's mask from the Red Wings—but Jason didn't wear it until *Friday the 13th Part III*.

22. WE CAN ALL JOKE ABOUT MOVIES BEING BASED ON BOARD GAMES LIKE *CLUE* AND *BATTLESHIP*, BUT EACH OF THE FOLLOWING FILMS FEATURES A BOARD GAME AS A PLOT POINT. NAME EACH BOARD GAME.

A. *Exorcist*

B. *Searching for Bobby Fischer*

C. *Sneakers*

D. *Bill & Ted's Bogus Journey*

23. ORIGINALLY SCHEDULED BY PIXAR FOR A SUMMER 2011 RELEASE, WHAT FILM WAS ULTIMATELY CANCELLED BY THE ANIMATION GIANT?

A. *frog*

B. *turtle*

C. *newt*

D. *worm*

22.

A. The Ouija board. In the movie, Linda Blair's Regan uses a Ouija board to speak with Captain Howdy.

B. Chess. It's based on the true story of a prodigy chess player, but not Bobby Fischer.

C. Scrabble. "TOO MANY SECRETS." The heroes use Scrabble to solve an anagram.

D. Clue, Twister, and even Battleship. Bill and Ted defeat Death every time.

23.

C. In 2010, Pixar cancelled the development of *newt*. The story followed two rare newts that needed to mate in order to save their species, even though they couldn't stand each other. Appropriate content for a children's film? Similarly themed animated films *Rio* and *Alpha and Omega* suggest otherwise, and possibly led to the Pixar project's demise.

24. TO PROTECT A FILM'S SECRETS, PRODUCTIONS SOMETIMES USE A FAKE WORKING TITLE. WHICH OF THE FOLLOWING FILMS WENT UNDER THE FAKE WORKING TITLE *BLUE HARVEST*?

A. *Superman II*

B. *Return of the Jedi*

C. *E.T. the Extra-Terrestrial*

D. *The Abyss*

25. SEQUELS SOMETIMES TAKE A WHILE TO SHOW UP. MATCH EACH ORIGINAL FILM TO ITS SEQUEL.

1. *Chinatown*	**A.** *Staying Alive*
2. *The Hustler*	**B.** *Gator*
3. *White Lightning*	**C.** *From Russia with Love*
4. *Saturday Night Fever*	**D.** *The Two Jakes*
5. *Dirty Harry*	**E.** *Magnum Force*
6. *Dr. No*	**F.** *The Color of Money*

24.

B. The third *Star Wars* film also went through an actual name change. George Lucas, who initially called his third installment *Revenge of the Jedi*, decided that Jedis don't seek revenge and opted instead for *Return of the Jedi*. The sixth film's name, *Revenge of the Sith*, alludes to *Jedi*'s original title. Speaking of allusions, the writers of *The Simpsons* gave their feature film debut the working title of *Yellow Harvest* as, what else, a joke.

25.

1. D; 2. F; 3. B; 4. A; 5. E; 6. C

The biggest gap between sequels on this list is between *The Hustler* and *The Color of Money* at 25 years. As for the shortest, *Dr. No* and *From Russia with Love* came out in 1962 and 1963 respectively. People couldn't get enough James Bond.

MUSIC

1. BY WHICH NAME WAS WILL SMITH KNOWN DURING HIS EARLY RAP CAREER?

2. WHO WAS SMITH'S HIP-HOP COLLABORATOR (AND OCCASIONAL TV FRIEND)?

3. WHICH OF THE FOLLOWING SINGERS GOT HIS STAGE NAME FROM A BILLBOARD ADVERTISING A HEARING-AID RETAILER?

A. Sting

B. Prince

C. Bono

D. Moby

4. HOW MANY KEYS ARE ON A STANDARD PIANO KEYBOARD?

1.

The Fresh Prince. He later starred on the TV show *The Fresh Prince of Bel-Air* (1990–96). At the time, few people would have predicted that the rapper would eventually be Oscar-nominated (*Ali*, 2001, and *The Pursuit of Happyness*, 2006).

2.

DJ Jazzy Jeff

3.

C. As the story goes, Bono (Paul David Hewson) was inspired by a Dublin hearing-aid shop called Bono Vox—Latin for "good voice."

4.

88 (52 white, 36 black)

5. GERMAN COMPOSER LUDWIG VAN BEETHOVEN BEGAN TO LOSE HIS SENSE OF WHAT WHEN HE WAS 28 YEARS OLD?

A. Hearing

B. Humor

C. Sight

D. Style

6. A HOST OF MUSICAL GENIUSES HAVE GONE TO AN EARLY GRAVE. BRIAN JONES (A FOUNDING MEMBER OF THE ROLLING STONES), JIMI HENDRIX, JANIS JOPLIN, JIM MORRISON, KURT COBAIN, AND AMY WINEHOUSE ALL PASSED AWAY AT THE SAME YOUNG AGE. HOW OLD WERE THEY?

7. OZZY OSBOURNE BECAME FAMOUS WITH WHICH HEAVY METAL BAND?

A. AC/DC

B. Black Sabbath

C. Iron Maiden

D. Judas Priest

5.

A. At around age 28, Beethoven developed a severe case of tinnitus and began to lose his hearing. This did not affect his ability to compose music, but it made conducting concerts increasingly difficult. According to one story, at the premiere of his Ninth Symphony when he was 54 years old, he had to be turned around to see the applause of the audience because he couldn't hear it.

6.

They were 27. If you're a rock star and you're about to turn 27, you might want to consider taking a year off.

7.

B. B is for Black Sabbath, but it's also for bat—as in the bat whose head Ozzy legendarily bit off when a fan tossed it onto the stage at a 1982 concert.

8. PUT THESE *AMERICAN IDOL* WINNERS IN ORDER FROM EARLIEST TO MOST RECENT.

   A. Kris Allen

   B. Fantasia Barrino

   C. David Cook

   D. Jordin Sparks

   E. Carrie Underwood

9. WHICH *AMERICAN IDOL* CONTESTANT HAS WON AN ACADEMY AWARD?

10. WHAT EVENTUALLY KILLED THE OLD LADY WHO SWALLOWED THE FLY?

   A. A cow

   B. A fly

   C. A horse

   D. A moose

11. TRUE OR FALSE?

Michael Jackson's "Thriller" video was nominated for an Academy Award.

8.

B. (Season 3), **E.** (Season 4), **D.** (Season 6), **C.** (Season 7), **A.** (Season 8)

9.

Jennifer Hudson (Best Supporting Actress 2006, *Dreamgirls*)

10.

C. A horse, of course!

11.

False. It wasn't nominated, but producers made sure it was eligible by giving it a one-week theatrical release in 1983, opening for the Disney movie *Fantasia*. Parents weren't too thrilled about their toddlers getting an eyeful of zombie action.

12. **WHICH COUNTRY SINGER IS KNOWN AS THE MAN IN BLACK?**

A. Clint Black

B. Garth Brooks

C. Johnny Cash

D. Hank Williams

13. **CAN YOU NAME THE SONG EACH OF THESE LYRICS COMES FROM?**

A. "Thunderbolt and lightning, very, very frightening."

B. "A singer in a smoky room, a smell of wine and cheap perfume."

C. "Hands, touching hands, reaching out, touching me, touching you."

D. "Well, I know that you're in love with him, 'cause I saw you dancin' in the gym."

E. "You start to scream, but terror takes the sound before you make it."

14. **CAN YOU NAME THE FIVE ORIGINAL MTV VJs?**

12.

C. Cash has been inducted into the Country Music Hall of Fame, the Rock and Roll Hall of Fame, the Gospel Music Hall of Fame, and the Rockabilly Hall of Fame.

13.

A. "Bohemian Rhapsody" (Queen)

B. "Don't Stop Believin'" (Journey)

C. "Sweet Caroline" (Neil Diamond)

D. "American Pie" (Don McLean)

E. "Thriller" (Michael Jackson)

14.

Alan Hunter, Mark Goodman, Nina Blackwood, Martha Quinn, and J. J. Jackson (who passed away in 2004). Nowadays, you can find the remaining VJs introducing 1980s hits 24 hours a day, 7 days a week on satellite radio...just like how they did it on MTV, when it still stood for Music Television.

15. WHO IS THE GREEK GOD OF MUSIC?

A. Apollo

B. Dionysus

C. Hermes

D. Zeus

16. WHICH LEGENDARY JAZZ MUSICIAN WAS KNOWN AS "SATCHMO"?

A. Duke Ellington

B. Charlie Parker

C. Glenn Miller

D. Louis Armstrong

17. LIONEL RICHIE ORIGINALLY RECORDED "ENDLESS LOVE" AS A DUET WITH DIANA ROSS. ON HIS 2012 ALBUM *TUSKEGEE*, HE RECORDED A NEW VERSION WITH WHICH COUNTRY SINGER?

A. Faith Hill

B. Taylor Swift

C. Natalie Maines

D. Shania Twain

15.

A. Apollo was not only the god of music—he was also the god of healing, the sun, and poetry, to name a few. If you got this question right, lift your glass to Dionysus, god of wine, parties, and festivals.

16.

D. When Armstrong was a child, his friends called him Satchelmouth because they thought his mouth was as large as a satchel. (He was also sometimes called Gatemouth. With friends like that, who needs enemies?) A music journalist mispronounced the moniker, shortening it to "Satchmo." Armstrong loved the name and quickly adopted it.

17.

D. Richie's tenth studio album is comprised of his old hit songs reinterpreted as duets. Some guests include Willie Nelson, Darius Rucker of Hootie and the Blowfish, and Jimmy Buffett. Wisely, he chose not to include his daughter Nicole's friend Paris Hilton.

18. MANY FAMOUS ROCK 'N' ROLL BANDS WENT BY DIFFERENT NAMES BEFORE THEY MADE IT BIG. CAN YOU IDENTIFY THE FORMER NAMES OF THESE BANDS?

1. The Beatles   **A.** Feedback; The Hype

2. Journey   **B.** Golden Gate Rhythm Section

3. KISS   **C.** The Pendletones

4. The Rolling Stones   **D.** Satan's Jesters

5. U2   **E.** Wicked Lester

19. JOHN WILLIAMS, WINNER OF MULTIPLE OSCARS, GRAMMYS, GOLDEN GLOBES, AND EMMY AWARDS, AND COMPOSER OF SOME OF THE MOST RECOGNIZABLE FILM SCORES IN HISTORY, ALSO COMPOSED THE THEME MUSIC FOR THREE OF THESE FOUR EVENTS. WHICH OF THE FOLLOWING DID NOT AT ONE TIME HAVE A THEME COMPOSED BY WILLIAMS?

A. Olympics

B. Academy Awards show

C. *NBC Nightly News*

D. *NBC Sunday Night Football*

18.

1. C; 2. B; 3. E; 4. D; 5. A.

19.

B. Although Williams is the second-most-nominated person in Academy Awards history—47 nods as of 2012—he has never composed the music for the show. (In case you're wondering, Walt Disney has the most nominations, with 59.)

20. WHAT DO ROCK 'N' ROLLER JERRY LEE LEWIS AND MASTER OF THE MACABRE EDGAR ALLAN POE HAVE IN COMMON?

21. THE WOODSTOCK MUSIC AND ART FESTIVAL WAS HELD AUGUST 15–18, 1969, NOT IN WOODSTOCK BUT IN BETHEL, NEW YORK, 40 MILES AWAY. WOODSTOCK WAS SUPPOSED TO HOST THE FESTIVAL, BUT WHEN RUMORS SPREAD THAT ATTENDANCE COULD REACH A MILLION PEOPLE, THE CITY BACKED OUT. DAIRY FARMER MAX YASGUR SAVED THE CONCERT BY HOSTING IT IN A FIELD AT HIS FARM. WHAT CROP WAS GROWING IN THAT FIELD?

A. Alfalfa

B. Cabbage

C. Corn

D. Marijuana

20.

Each married his 13-year-old cousin.

21.

A. Alfalfa is the answer, but the free-spirited flower children who attended the concert might have preferred one of the other options.

22. TRUE OR FALSE?

Piano is the shortened form of another word.

23. MATCH EACH MUSICAL GROUP TO THE FILM OR TV SHOW THAT INSPIRED ITS NAME.

1. Duran Duran

2. T'Pau

3. Save Ferris

4. The Fratellis

5. Black Rebel Motorcycle Club

6. Atreyu

7. Thompson Twins

A. *The Wild One*

B. *Ferris Bueller's Day Off*

C. *Barbarella*

D. *Star Trek: The Original Series*

E. *The Adventures of Tintin*

F. *The Goonies*

G. *The Neverending Story*

24. WHICH WAS THE FIRST SONG USED TO DEVELOP MP3s?

A. Suzanne Vega's "Tom's Diner"

B. The Moody Blues' "Nights in White Satin"

C. Procol Harum's "A Whiter Shade of Pale"

D. The Beatles' "Blackbird"

22.

True. *Pianoforte* is Italian for "quiet" (*piano*) and "loud" (*forte*), and refers to the ability to play the notes quiet or loud or anywhere in between. If the person playing the piano is terrible, you'd probably prefer them to play piano *piano*.

23.

1. C; 2. D; 3. B; 4. F; 5. A; 6. G; 7. E

Dr. Durand Durand, T'Pau, the Fratellis, Atreyu, and the Thompson Twins are all characters in their respective works. "Save Ferris" was a fundraising campaign, and the Black Rebels were—you guessed it—a motorcycle club.

24.

A. The theory behind the development of MP3s dates back to 1894 with the concept of auditory masking, or when tones block the sound of other tones. It only took them 100 years to figure it out.

25. THE PHRASE "FRIENDS WITH BENEFITS" WAS INTRODUCED BY ALANIS MORISSETTE IN WHICH OF HER HIT SONGS?

A. "All I Really Want"

B. "You Learn"

C. "Head Over Feet"

D. "Ironic"

26. WHICH CD WAS THE FIRST ONE MANUFACTURED IN THE U.S.?

A. Billy Joel's *52nd Street*

B. Bruce Springsteen's *Born in the U.S.A.*

C. Cyndi Lauper's *She's So Unusual*

D. Blondie's *The Hunter*

27. TRUE OR FALSE?

All three members of ZZ Top have beards.

25.

C. The word choices Morissette made with "Head Over Feet" didn't pay off as well in "Ironic." As it turns out, she used the word ironic incorrectly in the song, referring to annoying coincidences rather than ironic situations. Is that ironic, or is it an annoying coincidence?

26.

B. Joel's 1978 album was the first to be available for sale on CD in Japan in 1982, but Springsteen's most iconic album was aptly named—it was the first made in the U.S.A. starting in September 1984.

27.

False. Billy Gibbons and Dusty Hill sport the iconic long beards; amazingly, drummer Frank Beard rocks only a moustache (except for that phase in the '90s when he had a *small* beard).

POLITICS & WORLD NEWS

1. WHO IS THE ONLY PRESIDENT NEVER TO HAVE WON A GENERAL ELECTION?

2. UNDER PRESIDENTIAL SUCCESSION LAW, WHO IS NEXT IN LINE FOR THE PRESIDENCY AFTER THE VICE PRESIDENT AND THE SPEAKER OF THE HOUSE?

A. President pro tempore of the Senate

B. Secretary of state

C. Secretary of defense

D. Secretary of the Treasury

3. TRUE OR FALSE?

The American flag must be burned if it touches the ground.

1.

Gerald Ford. Ford was nominated for and ultimately became vice president when Spiro Agnew resigned in 1973. After President Richard Nixon resigned in 1974, Ford became president. In 1976, he narrowly defeated Ronald Reagan for the Republican nomination for president but eventually lost to Jimmy Carter.

2.

A. When President Andrew Johnson was impeached in 1868, he had no vice president—Senate president pro tempore Benjamin Franklin Wade was next in line. Wade was a radical, and historians believe that Johnson was tried and acquitted mostly to keep Wade out of the White House. Shortly afterward, the Speaker and president pro tempore were removed from the line of succession. When they were ultimately restored in 1947, the Speaker and president pro tempore were placed third and fourth, respectively.

3.

False. Out of respect, it shouldn't touch the ground, but there's no mandate that it be burned if this happens.

4. IN 2013, SENATOR RAND PAUL MADE NEWS WHEN HE FILIBUSTERED CONGRESS BY TALKING FOR **12** HOURS AND **52** MINUTES, MARKING THE NINTH-LONGEST FILIBUSTER ON RECORD. WHO HOLDS THE RECORD FOR THE LONGEST FILIBUSTER OF THE U.S. CONGRESS?

A. Barney Frank

B. Ron Paul

C. Ruth Baker Pratt

D. Strom Thurmond

5. HOW MANY AMENDMENTS ARE THERE TO THE U.S. CONSTITUTION?

A. 19

B. 23

C. 27

D. 31

6. WHAT COLOR IS THE BOTTOM STRIPE ON THE AMERICAN FLAG? YOU DON'T NEED THE COLORS LISTED, DO YOU?

4.

D. The late South Carolina senator Strom Thurmond spoke against the 1957 Civil Rights Act for 24 hours and 18 minutes. What a waste of time. At least Rand Paul was questioning our government's use of drones on American soil.

5.

C. The last amendment added to the Constitution enacted new rules about when salary changes for members of Congress can take effect. The amendment was submitted to the states for ratification in 1789 and adopted in 1992. How's that for progress?

6.

Red. There are thirteen alternating stripes, seven red and six white. But do you know how many stars are in the bottom row? (Six. Five rows of six stars alternate with four rows of five stars, for a grand total of 50 stars.)

7. WHICH OF THE FOLLOWING IS HEADQUARTERED IN LANGLEY, VIRGINIA?

A. Central Intelligence Agency (CIA)

B. Department of Homeland Security (DHS)

C. Federal Bureau of Investigation (FBI)

D. Internal Revenue Service (IRS)

8. WHO RAN AGAINST GEORGE W. BUSH FOR THE PRESIDENCY IN 2004?

A. Hillary Clinton

B. John Kerry

C. Al Gore

D. Joe Biden

9. WHAT WAS THE TITLE BESTOWED ON KATE MIDDLETON WHEN SHE MARRIED PRINCE WILLIAM?

A. Duchess of Cambridge

B. Duchess of Cornwall

C. Duchess of York

D. Princess Catherine

7.

A. The headquarters of the other three agencies are all in Washington, D.C. Spies do tend to be loners.

8.

B. Between the 2000 election and 2004 election, only three states changed their party alignment. New Mexico and Iowa voted for Al Gore in 2000 and then for Bush in 2004, and New Hampshire voted for Bush in 2000 and then for Kerry in 2004. Bush's voting numbers were the highest until President Barack Obama's totals in 2008 and 2012, but he still retains the highest amount for any Republican presidential nominee.

9.

A. Judging by tabloid shorthand, you might've thought she followed in Madonna, Cher, and Adele's footsteps to become simply Kate.

10. WHO WAS THE FIRST U.S. PRESIDENT TO BE IMPEACHED?

A. Andrew Johnson

B. James K. Polk

C. Richard Nixon

D. Bill Clinton

11. WHO WAS THE DIRECTOR OF THE FBI FOR ALMOST HALF OF THE 20TH CENTURY?

A. Winston Churchill

B. Allen Dulles

C. J. Edgar Hoover

D. Howard Hughes

12. WHICH CELEBRITY WAS AL GORE'S COLLEGE ROOMMATE AT HARVARD?

A. Billy Crystal

B. Tommy Lee Jones

C. Steven Spielberg

D. Henry Winkler

10.

A. Johnson was Abraham Lincoln's vice president and succeeded Lincoln following his assassination. Johnson was impeached by the House of Representatives, though the act failed in the U.S. Senate. (Remember question #2?) Johnson was impeached for violating the Tenure of Office Act that had been enacted the year before, which he vetoed and Congress passed anyway.

11.

C. Hoover was appointed in 1924 and held the position until his death in 1972. He began the world's largest fingerprint file, a scientific detection lab, and the FBI National Academy, among many other accomplishments. He also used the organization's secret files to benefit himself by blackmailing politicians to secure his powerful position.

12.

B. Can you imagine the former vice president and Agent K from *Men in Black* hanging out between classes? Doesn't seem too far-fetched.

13. TRUE OR FALSE?

The only people who appear on common
U.S. currency are presidents.

14. WHAT IS THE OFFICIAL TITLE FOR THE POLITICAL LEADER OF AUSTRALIA?

A. President

B. Prime Minister

C. Chancellor

D. Supreme Commander

15. WHAT DOES THE "S" IN HARRY S. TRUMAN STAND FOR?

A. Shipp

B. Stuyvesant

C. Solomon

D. It didn't stand for anything

13.

False. Alexander Hamilton appears on the $10 bill, and Benjamin Franklin is on the $100 bill. We all know that Franklin was a real Renaissance man (an author, scientist, postmaster, and inventor, among other things), but what did Hamilton do? Only served as the first Secretary of the Treasury and opened the U.S. Mint.

14.

B. But Australia is a part of the Commonwealth realms, which makes Queen Elizabeth II of England the nation's reigning monarch. Her full title there is Elizabeth the Second, by the Grace of God, Queen of Australia and Her other Realms and Territories, Head of the Commonwealth. Conversely, the position of Prime Minister is not mentioned in the Constitution of Australia and is merely an unwritten custom.

15.

D. The "S" did not stand for a name, though it alluded to both of Truman's grandfather's names—Anderson Shipp Truman and Solomon Young.

16. WHO WAS THE ONLY UNITED STATES PRESIDENT TO REMAIN A BACHELOR WHILE IN OFFICE?

A. James Buchanan

B. John Tyler

C. Benjamin Harrison

D. Millard Fillmore

17. HOW MANY STARS OF THE 1987 SCI-FI FILM *PREDATOR* WENT ON TO BECOME STATE GOVERNORS?

18. FOR HOW LONG DID VICE PRESIDENTIAL NOMINEE SARAH PALIN SERVE AS GOVERNOR OF ALASKA?

A. 965 days

B. 156 weeks

C. 48 months

D. 6 years

P
O
L
I
T
I
C
S

&

W
O
R
L
D

N
E
W
S

16.

A. While Buchanan was the fifteenth president of the United States, he was engaged to Ann Caroline Coleman. Buchanan was extremely busy with his political work during their engagement, so Ann broke it off. She died shortly thereafter. Buchanan's niece Harriet Lane was the lady of the house during his term as president.

17.

Two. Arnold Schwarzenegger went on to become the Governator of California; professional-wrestler Jesse "The Body" Ventura went on to become governor of Minnesota. *Saturday Night Live* writer and star Al Franken became a senator for Minnesota as well. Minnesotans must like their politicians good and famous.

18.

A. Palin was governor from December 4, 2006, until she resigned on July 26, 2009. For comparison, the first time Tina Fey parodied the politician on *Saturday Night Live* was September 13, 2008, and the last time was May 8, 2011—a span of 967 days!

19. WHICH OF THE FOLLOWING MOVIES DID PRESIDENT RONALD REAGAN NOT STAR IN?

A. *The Voice of the Turtle*

B. *Hellcats of the Navy*

C. *Girls on Probation*

D. *Million Dollar Baby*

20. WHICH BRITISH RULER'S SKELETON WAS DISCOVERED UNDER A PARKING LOT IN 2012?

A. Henry VIII

B. Richard III

C. Lord Fauntleroy

D. King Ralph

19.

Trick question: Ronnie was in all of them! *Million Dollar Baby* is also the title of a 1941 film about a department store worker who is given—you guessed it—a million dollars. It's more like *Shopgirl* meets *It Could Happen to You* than the 2004 Clint Eastwood-directed boxing film. Don't be so surprised. Reagan once starred opposite a chimpanzee in *Bedtime for Bonzo*.

20.

B. Now that Richard III's remains have been found, historians seek to further challenge previously held ideas brought about by William Shakespeare's play and his Tudor successors. It was once thought that Richard III was hunchbacked; now it appears he merely had a curved spine.

1. WHICH COMEDIAN FAMOUSLY RIFFED ABOUT THE "SEVEN WORDS YOU CAN NEVER SAY ON TELEVISION" WAY BACK IN 1972?

A. Bill Cosby

B. Sam Kinison

C. Richard Pryor

D. George Carlin

2. WHICH FORMER PRESIDENT WAS INVITED TO MAKE A GUEST APPEARANCE ON THE SERIES FINALE OF *CHEERS*?

A. Bill Clinton

B. George H. W. Bush

C. Ronald Reagan

D. Jimmy Carter

1.

D. These days, you can actually say one of the dirty words on network television and three of them on basic cable. But of course, all of them regularly appear on premium cable, and none of them will appear here.

2.

A. President Clinton passed on the offer, so a different type of president took his place—Brandon Tartikoff (then head of NBC programming). He was joined by cartoonist Garry Trudeau in cameos for the final episode, which aired May 20, 1993.

3. WHICH FAMOUS *SATURDAY NIGHT LIVE* ALUM GOT HER START ON THE REALITY SHOW *THE JOE SCHMO SHOW*?

A. Amy Poehler

B. Kristen Wiig

C. Tina Fey

D. Maya Rudolph

4. WHICH OF THE FOLLOWING SUPERSTARS GOT HIS START ON TV, MAKING GUEST APPEARANCES IN *ANOTHER WORLD*, *GROWING PAINS*, *DALLAS*, AND *21 JUMP STREET*?

A. Leonardo DiCaprio

B. Johnny Depp

C. Brad Pitt

D. George Clooney

5. WHAT IS THE NAME OF THE HOLIDAY CELEBRATION COINED ON THE TV SHOW *SEINFELD*?

3.

B. Spike TV's reality show was about one guy that didn't realize he was on a fake reality show. Wiig was one of the actors in on the scam, as was David Hornsby. You might know him better as Rickety Cricket on *It's Always Sunny in Philadelphia*. Not too shabby for two former Joe Schmos.

4.

C. DiCaprio had a major role near the end of *Growing Pains*' run, and Depp was the main attraction on *21 Jump Street*, but Pitt was a guest star on all those shows. He also appeared on *Friends* as a former classmate of Jennifer Aniston's Rachel. Were you aware that they used to be married in real life?

5.

Festivus. Those looking to celebrate the "Festivus for the Rest of Us" should plan on the traditional "Airing of Grievances" and "Feats of Strength," in which the head of household must be pinned in a wrestling match. An unadorned aluminum pole is put up instead of a Christmas tree.

6. IN THE TELEVISION SHOW *PARKS AND RECREATION*, THE FICTIONAL CITY OF PAWNEE IS LOCATED IN WHAT STATE?

A. Ohio

B. Pennsylvania

C. Iowa

D. Indiana

7. MATCH THESE TV SERIES TO THE CITIES IN WHICH THEY ARE SET.

1. *CSI: Crime Scene Investigation*

2. *Grey's Anatomy*

3. *House*

4. *Law & Order (the original)*

5. *NCIS*

A. Las Vegas

B. New York City

C. Princeton, New Jersey

D. Seattle

E. Washington, D.C.

6.

D. Councilwoman Leslie Knope, as portrayed by Amy Poehler, truly loves the city of Pawnee. Her husband is a close second...or maybe waffles are.

7.

1. A; 2. D; 3. C; 4. B; 5. E.

A trivia tidbit for you: There have been four American spin-offs of the original *Law and Order*: *Special Victims Unit*, *Criminal Intent*, *Trial by Jury*, and *L.A.* Versions of the show have also been produced in Russia, France, and the United Kingdom.

8. *STAR TREK* **HAS HAD MANY INCARNATIONS ON TELEVISION. WHICH RUN HAD THE MOST EPISODES?**

A. *The Original Series*

B. *The Next Generation*

C. *Deep Space Nine*

D. *Voyager*

E. *Enterprise*

9. **WHEN WAS THE FIRST-EVER TELEVISED BASEBALL GAME?**

A. 1939

B. 1951

C. 1948

D. 1942

10. **WHICH OF THESE ACTORS WAS NEVER A PART OF THE *SATURDAY NIGHT LIVE* CAST?**

A. Alec Baldwin

B. Robert Downey, Jr.

C. Will Ferrell

D. Adam Sandler

8.

B. It was close, but *The Next Generation* aired 178 episodes, plus four theatrical films. *Deep Space Nine* aired 176, *Voyager* aired 172, and *Enterprise* aired 98. *Star Trek: The Original Series* had only 79 episodes, but it did get four spin-off series, plus eight movies (and counting). Captain Kirk for the win!

9.

A. On May 17, 1939, the game between Princeton and Columbia was played at Baker Field and broadcast on W2XBS. Princeton won 2-1, but we all know TV really won.

10.

A. As of 2013, Baldwin has hosted *SNL* a record 16 times, but he was never a cast member.

TELEVISION

11. JON STEWART HAS MADE A GLOBAL IMPACT AS HOST OF *THE DAILY SHOW* ON COMEDY CENTRAL, AND THE SHOW HAS HELPED LAUNCH THE CAREERS OF SEVERAL FORMER CAST MEMBERS AS WELL. WHICH OF THE FOLLOWING FUNNY FOLKS DID NOT GET HIS OR HER START ON *THE DAILY SHOW*?

A. Steve Carell

B. Stephen Colbert

C. Ed Helms

D. Amy Sedaris

12. WHICH OSCAR-NOMINATED ACTOR IS RUMORED TO HAVE HATED THE '80S TV SHOW HE STARRED ON SO MUCH THAT HE LIT HIS UNDERWEAR ON FIRE IN AN ATTEMPT TO GET FIRED?

A. George Clooney

B. Johnny Depp

C. Tom Hanks

D. Will Smith

187

QUESTIONS

11.

D. The actress, comedian, and author has appeared on Stewart's show as a guest, but she was never a regular contributor.

12.

B. When Depp joined the cast of *21 Jump Street* in 1987, he did so believing it would be for only one season. When the show became a hit, he was stuck. Eager to be taken more seriously, Depp got creative in trying to escape his contract, but it took four long seasons before he was finally free to leave. He apparently got over his distaste for the role, however, and good-naturedly made a cameo in the 2012 movie based on the series.

13. WHO COHOSTED THE FIRST SEASON OF *AMERICAN IDOL* WITH RYAN SEACREST?

A. Brian Dunkleman

B. Jason Kennedy

C. Ben Lyons

D. Catt Sadler

14. WHAT ARE THE NAMES OF THE TWO OLD MEN WHO SIT IN THE BALCONY ON *THE MUPPET SHOW*?

A. Aspin and Ludsthorp

B. Chilton and Gerard

C. Hawkins and Nigel

D. Waldorf and Statler

15. PUT THESE REALITY SHOWS IN THE ORDER IN WHICH THEY DEBUTED, FIRST TO LAST:

A. *American Idol*

B. *Dancing with the Stars*

C. *The Real World*

D. *Survivor*

E. *Top Chef*

13.

A. Dunkleman left the show after the first season with his career in ruins. Seacrest went on to become an entertainment mogul.

14.

D. The ornery octogenarians enjoy heckling the other Muppets from the best seats in the house. Their names are based on hotels in New York: the Waldorf–Astoria and the Statler Hilton.

15.

C. (1992); **D.** (2000); **A.** (2002); **B.** (2005); **E.** (2006)

16. **WHAT NAME DID THE CORE GROUP OF FRIENDS USE TO REFER TO THEMSELVES ON THE SERIES *BUFFY THE VAMPIRE SLAYER* (1997–2003)?**

A. The Badanovs

B. The Felix Faith

C. The Scooby Gang

D. The Underdog Squad

17. **TGIF WAS ABC'S FRIDAY NIGHT BLOCK OF FAMILY-FRIENDLY SITCOMS. WHICH OF THESE SHOWS WAS NEVER UNDER THE "THANK GOODNESS IT'S FUNNY" BRAND?**

A. *Perfect Strangers*

B. *Dinosaurs*

C. *Webster*

D. *Hangin' with Mr. Cooper*

16.

C. Buffy, Willow, Xander, and Giles formed the core of the Scooby Gang, or the Scoobies. The spooky goings-on in Sunnydale, California, influenced today's vampire, werewolf, and supernatural craze.

17.

C. TGIF started in 1989, and although *Webster* aired on Fridays in 1987, it moved elsewhere on the schedule to make room for *Full House* the next year. The first official set of shows included *Full House*, *Family Matters*, *Perfect Strangers*, and *Just the Ten of Us*. How many of their theme songs can you still sing?